Accomplish the Impossible

The Six Secrets of
Sustainability and Transformation
for Business, Art, Science & Life

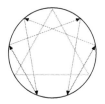

Steffan Soule

Revealing Wisdom
Hidden in the Enneagram

ATOM Press
Mercer Island, Washington

ATOM Press
2452 - 60th Ave SE
Mercer Island, WA 98040
www.accomplishtheimpossible.com

ISBN 978-0-9842405-1-7

Library of Congress Control Number 2010910441

Library of Congress Subject Headings:
Enneagram
Success in business
Organizational effectiveness
Efficiency
Sustainability
Self-actualization (Psychology)
System theory

Printed on Acid-free paper
Author photo by Tom Woodward
First Edition 1.0

To all those who see the invisible
for they can do the impossible.

Contents

Chapter 7

Chapter 8

Chapter 9

Chapter 10

Figures

But the very fact that there are *two* of us changes everything; the task does not become *twice* as easy, no: from being impossible it becomes possible. It's as if, to measure the distance from a star to our planet, you gave me *one* known point on the surface of the globe: the calculus is impossible. Give me a second point, it becomes possible, because then I can construct the triangle.

Rene Daumal, *Mount Analogue*

CHAPTER 1

A Magician's Guide to True Magic

I am passionate about two things in my life that may not seem related, but really are—magic, and something called the Nine Term Symbol. I discovered the joy of magic tricks long before I discovered the mystery and magic of the NTS. When I was four years old, I saw a magician for the first time and was astonished by what he did. He put an empty cylinder on a table, and then pulled things out of it; I couldn't believe it.

I went up to his table at the end of the show, to say hello, but when I placed my hand on his table, my hand sank down into an invisible chamber. He gently grabbed my hand, put a finger to his lips, and said, "Shhhhhh!" I realized the things he had pulled out of his cylinder had been in a hiding place in the table, and I was so excited to have discovered his secret.

I went home and immediately started trying to imitate him. I put on a magic show and tried to amaze my father; unfortunately, my show was not quite as amazing as I had hoped it would be. So I gave up magic for a while. But then when I was twelve I saw my friend take a playing card and throw it into the air, where it vanished, and I was intrigued all over again. My friend was part of a magician's club, and I joined it right away, too.

The first coin trick I learned was all about psychology. There is a suggestibility factor in people that is huge; you communicate more with your eyes than you think. For example, in a coin trick, you need to follow the coin with your eyes to where you are trying to make people believe it has gone, even though you have left it behind. You have to believe it yourself, just a little bit, so that other people believe it, too.

In learning magic tricks I was not interested in tricking people; instead, I was interested in creating amazement and wonder. The pure sense of wonder I experienced when I watched the performance of an astounding mystery lead me to want to create these effects myself. A person might say that magicians use psychology to trick people and fool them. This was not what I was after, although the psychology of it did fascinate me. I learned that people see things in certain patterns and in certain ways, and I wanted to know more about what those patterns were.

To be clear from the start, the type of magic I am talking about has nothing to do with the so called occult or black magic. In fact, such subjects are unrelated and of no interest to me. Instead, my magic is a blend of psychology, mental acuity, and physical skill—always done with a goal to entertain and inspire joy. Magic is a performing art like theatre or dance.

The feeling of wonder was so enchanting to me that I was compelled to explore it in depth. Along with wonder came the realization that I did not know much about the laws affecting the world around me. Magicians need to understand laws of physics in order to create effective illusions, but when you are enchanted with wonder, you want to learn the laws just to explore the physical universe. And then, no matter how deep or far we look, there are many phenomena that are incomprehensible and remain a mystery, so the wonder continues.

As a young person, I noticed that the grown ups around me—my teachers, my parents and all those responsible for my education—did not even know or understand most of these laws. Take electricity as an example. We use it every day, and yet it has not been fully explained by science. This lack of understanding was also mysterious to me. It clashed with an innate sense I had. I assumed that when I grew up, I would understand the world; I would know the meaning of life.

My father was an earth scientist and my mother was a music teacher. We used to go backpacking in the wilderness for weeks. On those trips I gained an appreciation for singing harmonies around the campfire and the vast ecosystems of nature. While I was growing up, I often had a feeling that the universe was full of glorious mystery and wonder, and that we were all unique. I just knew that there was a higher intelligence, one that could connect with us and that we could relate to. I wanted to find the answer to why we are here on this Earth, and how we are meant to be. From this, I was hoping for the power to manifest who I really was and what I really wanted to do with my life.

I saw that science was about discovering natural laws. Magicians manipulate ideas and objects in ways that appear to defy natural laws. They need to understand the laws as well as how their audiences will perceive them. When a magician floats a rose in mid air, the observer may say, "Where's the string?" So the magician must go further, passing a hoop over the floating rose to disprove the common theories arising in the minds of the spectators. In pursuit of my interests, I naturally developed a wish to go deeper than ordinary appearances and find some real secrets. I was seeking, and I had no idea what I would find.

When I was 17, I acquired two very crucial things—a car and a book titled *In Search of the Miraculous*. I drove with the book, a tent, and a sleeping bag to the farthest northern stretch of beach in Washington called Shi Shi Beach, which is a Native American name—the Makah Indians still live there. I feel it is one of the most special places in the world to visit: there is magic in the air. It was November, it was cold, and it rained most of the time I was camping. I spent my time reading the book, listening to the ocean, and looking out to sea from where I tried to stay dry in my tent.

I read the whole book over three days. I could not understand it all; much of it went over my head, but I was fascinated. The author, whose name is Ouspensky, talked about the enneagram, which is the symbol I call the Nine Term Symbol (NTS). He explained how his teacher, Gurdjieff, understood the rules of the universe and how they play out in this wonderful and intricate symbol with a circle, six lines and a triangle.

I understood the symbol immediately—this was just what I had been looking for! After all, I believed that the world could be magical and that there were universal patterns of physical laws that we do not understand. I believed in the potential for higher consciousness, and I believed that this symbol represented a scientific method by which my being could evolve and connect with that higher intelligence I had been seeking.

I realized that we are not all blind, as I was beginning to think. Instead, we just see small parts when the world is made up of wholes. We tend to see only part of any picture. This is what enables magicians to trick us. The magic of the NTS is that it reveals how the parts relate to and support the whole. It shows the whole picture.

As time went by, and as I learned how to use the symbol in my daily life, I couldn't believe how perfectly the symbol worked. I started seeing how it could be used everywhere, in any situation, and to this day have never stopped. I had it in mind in everything I did, whether personal or professional, and time and time again it showed the process I needed to follow to accomplish what I wanted to, whether something great like learning an advanced magic routine, or something mundane like buying a car.

If you want to convey a sense of wonder (such as performing a magic trick), you have to use language, posture, gesture, tone and voice in harmony together. To me, this is like the NTS—a number of things happening at the same time in harmony. But the NTS is even more magical to me than my magic. If you are in my audience, you might be astonished to see me produce a white dove out of thin air. But this is an illusion. The power of the NTS is not an illusion—it's real.

I am now a professional magician, highly skilled in my craft. From the time I was a kid in a magician's club, I could see that some people succeed in processes and others do not—and this ability to succeed in process seemed crucial to success. Aware of this, I began to develop an intuition for what actions might lead to solutions, but I did not understand how it all worked until I found the NTS. The secrets I found have helped me make my passion and profession one and the same. They helped me master my art and run a successful performing arts business.

It was as I started to engage my art with the business world, where I had to collaborate and think creatively to survive, that I found I was working with a tool that continuously nudged me toward greater creativity, collaboration, critical thinking and citizenship combined. As you will see, the NTS encapsulates these because it is a symbol for evolutionary change. Since all transformations are processes, the NTS appears at first to be a model for process improvement, but in reality, it inspires us to reach for the inaccessible, the unobtainable, the impossible. As we follow its guidance we evolve in a positive direction. How it does this and why it works is addressed throughout this book. The NTS is a work of art that inspires an artistic and a scientific way of harmonizing with the qualities that move us to transform.

While I believe that business has much to learn from art, both thrive on efficiency. When we compare our intended results to what actually happens in life, if we are honest, we see that there must be forces in play that we do not control. We can not move efficiently to our goals in straight lines with no setbacks. The NTS shows us our place in this mystery, and it helps us harmonize with all of the forces so we can achieve our aims.

I enjoy sharing the ideas in this book; they have a positive effect. The NTS has changed my life and I believe the symbol can help you, too, especially in your business. The NTS is all about whole systems thinking. Conventional business thinking tries to fill the gap, but it fails because it misses key steps in the process. The NTS does not miss any steps. Instead, it takes you through a clear and refined process that will make you more effective and productive in every aspect of your work. It will accelerate your growth.

Every successful process follows the pattern I am about to describe. It is a master pattern for living your passion, broadening your creativity and perfecting your expertise.

CHAPTER 2

How the NTS Works

Harnessing the power of the NTS is simply a matter of understanding how it describes the forces at play in a process. Few people understand how systems thinking works. Even successful people often have a hit-or-miss experience with it—sometimes they are able to see an issue or challenge as part of a greater whole, but many times they do not. This can create less-than-excellent results. But the Nine Term Symbol (NTS for short) leads you through a clear, step-by-step whole systems approach to tackle almost any challenge, whether personal or professional.

There are three sides of "How the NTS Works": theory, practice and results. Although it may all appear to be theory at first, in this chapter we will focus on how to work with the NTS (practice) and how we can succeed when we work with it (results). The results or benefits of the NTS will increase as we understand what they are, so let's begin there.

The NTS system creatively encourages you to see the whole while simultaneously connecting the parts in new ways along proven lines of success. Once you see how every well-managed process fits into this elegant, universal design, you will use its power to elevate your processes, increase your efficiency, share your insights with others, create new works, and propel yourself to mastery. To do this, you are going to have to start to access your magical mind.

What is the magical mind? When our minds are filled with wonder and we intentionally focus our attention on understanding a mystery, we begin to access what I call the magical mind. The mind has intuitive powers, the power to relate with what is unknowable. As a magician, I have tested this theory in the field at corporate and family events for thousands of people over many years. I have verified for myself and proven time and time again that there is a special creative power elicited through experiences with wonder, attention and ideas that cause our intelligences to stretch. I call any idea that helps our minds stay focused in this way a "magical idea" and I call the creativity and finer attention resulting from these experiences a product of our "magical mind."

The NTS contains magical ideas that connect our mind with patterns that incorporate the unknowable, and as we work with it intentionally during real life experiences, our magical mind automatically unfolds.

But to integrate the creative and intentional thinking that results, you must view your work in a new way. The NTS facilitates this too. As we engage our thinking with the patterns presented in this system, we strengthen our attention, our intuition, and our deeper intelligence. We develop our potential for synergy and synchronicity. We awaken our magical mind to a greater level of creativity—one that sees things in new ways and can comprehend magical ideas. And doing so is simply a matter of understanding an ancient symbol and how it describes the supporting forces within a process.

The symbol is a geometric figure known as the enneagram: a nine term symbol, or "NTS" for short. This figure is a circle divided into nine points. Three points are connected with a triangle. The remaining points make a six pointed figure and are connected by a pattern that repeats.

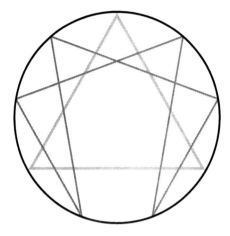

Figure 1 - The Nine Term Symbol (NTS)

A Straight Line View

There are many elements and aspects to a sustainable, recurring process or to an event in which transformation occurs. We tend to see things in straight lines, which we take as reality. As a magician, I show audiences that our ordinary reality is filled with illusions. The NTS will show that our world is not linear. Most process management systems depict lines connecting boxes alongside logical if-then-else-statements directing the ordinary, linear thinking mind to follow the events leading to a desired result. The NTS gives us a new approach to the elements of a process and to ordinary thinking at every turn.

Before we dig into the Nine Term Symbol, let's look at how the linear mind might picture the basics of the NTS. After presenting the wisdom of the NTS to groups with deep thinking individuals in seminars and workshops for many years, I have found that the linear approach can be helpful at the outset. Then, the fundamentals that follow become approachable from multiple perspectives.

Nine Term Symbol (NTS) basics begin by looking at six points.

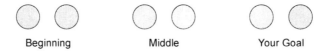

Beginning   Middle   Your Goal

Every process that is sustainable and involves change or growth has six points of concentration, six fundamental steps from beginning to end. The end is your aim or goal.

There are invisible connections between the points of a process that run in the background. They are depicted in the diagram below by the dotted and dashed lines between the six points.

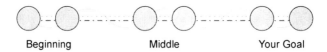

Beginning   Middle   Your Goal

Invisible connections connect the beginning, the middle and the ending in a specific pattern. These connections are made visible by the NTS. They comprise the Inner Compass (soon to be revealed), and below they are seen in a linear fashion.

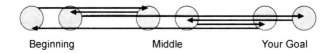

Beginning   Middle   Your Goal

To specify the pattern, we trace the six lines in the above diagram in the direction indicated by the arrows. As each line comes to its arrow, a new line begins just below it from the same point in a different direction. The lines connect the beginning with the middle, the middle with the step just after the beginning—where the third line begins and travels to the very end. From there, we turn back to the point right after the middle, next we go to a step just before the end, and as we close in on completing the process, we draw a line back to the beginning again.

Six lines connecting six separate points in six different ways. There is a far more effective way to view these connections. (I hope this comes as a relief.) But first, we will touch on three additional points.

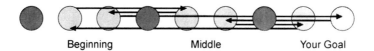

Beginning   Middle   Your Goal

Three mutually independent forces support every whole event, process or transformation. They enter the diagram above to make nine points. (The darker shade is for emphasis in this one instance.) These forces represent the context of a process and can provide an easy way for us to connect the understanding of our heart with the understanding of our intellect.

The NTS will show that we connect with nine points when we go from the beginning to the end of a process. But a sustainable process is not linear like we tend to think, left to right. The relationships between the three forces, the six fundamental points and the connecting lines are described by the Nine Term Symbol.

The Fundamentals of the NTS

The NTS is made up of three parts, all of which are crucial and each of which plays a different role. I call these three parts:

- The Circle Timeline (Circle)

- The Context Triangle (Triangle)

- The Inner Compass (Compass)

When they are placed together, they divide the Circle evenly into nine points. Three of these points make the Context Triangle, and the remaining six points belong to the recurring pattern called the Inner Compass.

As we will discuss later, these shapes represent mathematical laws significant for their relationship to processes. That is where the theory of the NTS will come into focus. Do not feel you have to memorize all the elements of the NTS, or even to fully understand them yet. We will go over them again in various ways in the coming chapters. This chapter is for you to get a feeling for the basics.

The magic of the NTS is in the powerful insights and applications we will have at our fingertips once we can use it for real situations. The magic comes from directing our attention along the lines of the pattern about to be revealed. This causes us to establish new connections according to entirely new principles, aligning us with wisdom from the harmonious relationships between the forces that move us toward completion. That's better than fighting against them—which so often happens when we are trying to solve a problem, and which keeps us from succeeding. These harmonious principles are the same forces that are already producing positive results when we are successful in our work.

Let's look at each of the three parts of the NTS, one by one, but keep in mind that learning the NTS from a book is like learning a dance from a choreographer who is limited to teaching the dance from the notes she has on paper. Dance is an ancient art, and yet no one knows the best way to notate dance. There are as many notation systems as there are choreographers. But they do it all the time—as best they can—and modern dances have the additional benefit of video archives along with written notations.

In this book, I am transmitting the dance of a process through the pages of a book. There is not one way to do this either. That is why there are several different approaches throughout this book, and fortunately there are videos available of the NTS at AccomplishTheImpossible.com. So, here we go—as best we can—the three parts of the NTS, one by one.

The Three Parts

The motion of a process is not linear—it's circular, and the NTS starts with a circle to symbolize that fact.

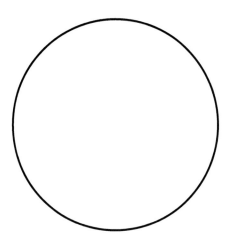

The Circle is the timeline of an event. It is the to-do list for the activity, the points that come together to make up the whole. Before a well-run process comes to an end, actions are launched that are intended to aim the process back to the beginning, to prepare it to begin again. As a process recurs, it can improve and evolve towards perfection. From this view, the circle can be seen as a spiral, not where the circles get tighter and tighter until they disappear, but like a slinky where the circles continue, one to the next. They support one another and make a spiral of continuous improvement—and it all starts with the Circle.

Whether you are making an NTS of a process, an expertise, an activity or a goal, each point will be labeled with a word (or a sentence) that describes one step of the experience. This is the most basic practical answer to the question of how the NTS works. It works when we use the nine points to label the steps of a process. But we must see the subtle aspects of the symbol in order to label all of the points in a way that will produce results.

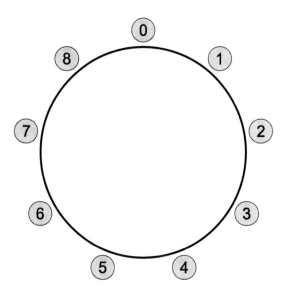

Figure 2 - The Circle Timeline (Circle)

Each of the nine points—start to finish, clockwise around the Circle—describes an activity, an action point or an element needed to complete the process.

If we look again at the nine points shown earlier in the linear view, we can see that they do indeed correspond.

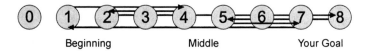

Beginning   Middle   Your Goal

The pairs of points labeled "beginning," "middle," and "your goal" are the exact same points as the ones on the Circle Timeline numbered 1,2,4,5,7 and 8.

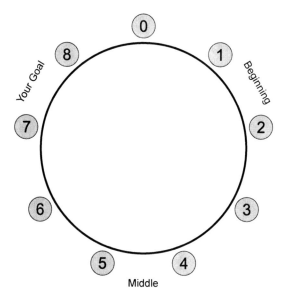

Now that we have our Circle Timeline with its nine points, we can consider the Triangle (points 0, 3, 6). Three supporting forces must be present for an activity to be sustainable, and this is symbolized by a triangle.

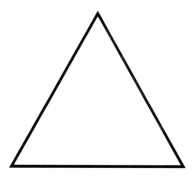

The Circle is your timeline, and the Triangle is the context of your process. The context includes the reasons for your process: the principle benefit to the world, who or what is being served, as well as external ingredients needed for doing the process.

Think of the points of the Triangle as values, inputs or sources that are needed for the process to exist in the first place. You could tell someone just these three points, and they would have an idea of what must be taking place, for example: "entertainment," "magician," "audience." They are ingredients of and reasons for a process that characterize the context of the process. They may be transformed during the process, but they contribute to and are not produced by the process, like "customers," "materials," and "maintenance." They are context oriented, which is why we refer to the triangle within the circle as "the Context Triangle."

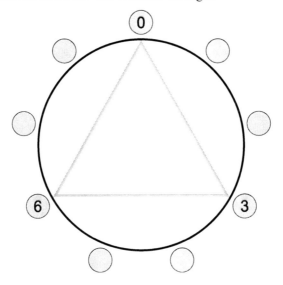

Figure 3 - The Context Triangle (Triangle)

The points of the Context Triangle can represent ideas that are flexible and even sometimes invisible to our ordinary way of thinking. The Context Triangle may represent human values as well as inputs or sources that may change or transform during the process. One of the points of the Context Triangle will likely represent who or what will grow or benefit. Another point might be labeled with ingredients.

The apex of the Context Triangle is the point where the process begins again. Activities we care about enough to examine usually serve us as a recurring process. There is flexibility here, but as we begin, for simplicity, the apex of the Context Triangle can be labeled with the overarching higher purpose to our work: our mission statement; that which brings everything together, the reconciling force.

In physics, triangles are known for their strength and stability because of the way they evenly distribute any force applied to their structure. In the NTS, you can think of the Context Triangle as evenly distributing three forces to every recurring activity.

ଓ ◇ ଉ

The final of the three parts is the Inner Compass, a six-pointed figure of interconnecting lines that make a recurring pattern—a pattern that repeats. It moves in the direction of the arrows to each of its points in succession. It travels from point 1 through the inside of the circle, comes near to the end of the Circle's sequential timeline at point 7, and then it joins back to its starting point.

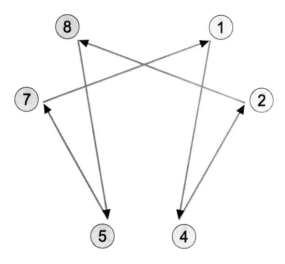

Figure 4 - The Inner Compass (Compass)

It is along the lines of this figure that the secrets of the Compass appear. I call them the Six Secrets, and one of the secrets corresponds to each line. Soon, they will act as a guide for mapping out our activities around the Circle Timeline. These Six Secrets of the Inner Compass are not named this way as a gimmick. Being a magician means knowing the difference between what is genuine and what is merely a distraction.

The word "inner" refers to the lines that live and move inside the Circle. As I said, they move in the direction of the arrows. Each line connects two of the external points of the Circle Timeline with one of the Six Secrets.

They are called "secrets" because they work in the background, are often overlooked and give us power when we consciously use them. Those who can see the Six Secrets can use them to connect the past and present with the future. They provide a way for us to find the bearing—not of an object in space, but of a necessary quality. The Inner Compass actually helps us find the bearing of six qualities and their position in relation to any process. When we bring these qualities into our work, at the right point, at the right time, we aid success. A compass is used to find direction and provide bearing, which gives us the simple name of this six pointed figure.

Now, remember the Circle Timeline? When we label an important process around the points of the Circle, we consider the pattern behind the activities by using the Inner Compass with its Six Secrets. This will soon come into full focus, but now that we have all three parts, let's discuss the different types of steps that occur as we travel from point to point around the Circle Timeline.

The types of steps of your process that are placed on the points of the Inner Compass differ from those placed at the points of the Context Triangle. The six points that make up the Compass are the most basic action points that need to be done in sequence to accomplish what it is that you want to do: your goal.

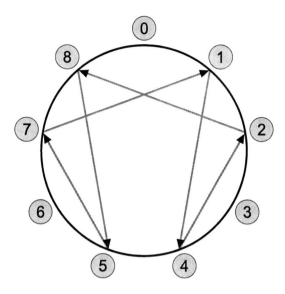

Figure 5 - The Compass within the Circle

You place the important values, inputs or sources at the points of the Context Triangle, and onto the points of the Compass you place the most basic functions of your process, all in succession, like a regular timeline, but clockwise rather than linearly.

Soon you will understand specific factors to consider as you place the steps of your process onto the points of the symbol. This will come from the Six Secrets of the Inner Compass. They supply the missing link to using this symbol as a tool for understanding process, and here, for the first time, they are revealed.

The Six Secrets of the Inner Compass:

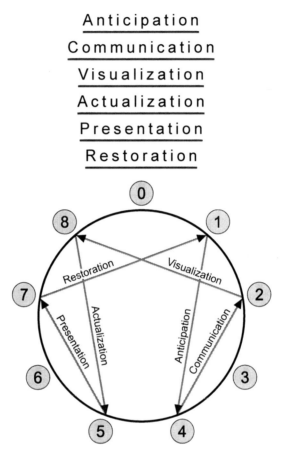

Anticipation

Communication

Visualization

Actualization

Presentation

Restoration

Figure 6 - NTS with the Six Secrets of the Inner Compass

This is where your magical mind comes into play—you will engage your magical mind to compare these Six Secrets of the Inner Compass, which work along the lines of 1-4-2-8-5-7-1, with the steps of your process. Since each secret runs between two specific points, you consider those two points in light of the secret that links them together. Of course you do this once you are involved with labeling the points of the Circle Timeline with the steps of your process. This book will guide you to create your own Nine Term Symbol. We will explore the meaning and significance of these Six Secrets in the chapters ahead. They are used to hone the diagram and help you arrive at the place of completion you pictured at the start of the process.

The Six Secrets will turn the key that unlocks your power to efficiently improve and control the quality of the points around the timeline of your Circle. These secrets, once understood, become a practical tool for unlimited mastery. You may have encountered each of these secrets in separate compartments. For example, there are dozens of books that talk about the importance of visualization. Communication is the bread and butter of corporate seminars. Presentation becomes important as a project nears completion. And actualization has become a buzzword for action. But each of these is only one part of a greater whole and only shows us part of the bigger picture. This is illustrated by the Eastern parable of the six blind men and the elephant.

Six blind men encounter an elephant for the first time. The first blind man touches the side of the elephant and reports that it is smooth like a wall. The second blind man puts his hands around the trunk of the elephant. He says the elephant is like a snake. The third blind man touches the tusk of the elephant and says the elephant is sharp like a spear. The fourth blind man touches the leg of the elephant and thinks it is a tree. The fifth blind man reaches out his hands, touches the ear of the elephant and tells everyone that the elephant is like a piece of leather. The sixth blind man grabs onto the tail of the elephant and exclaims that an elephant would make a good rope.

We know that they must put all the parts together to find out what an elephant is really like. But just as each of the blind men sees only a part and takes it for the whole, we often see each of the Six Secrets: Anticipation, Communication, Visualization, Actualization, Presentation and Restoration as the overall picture. They are not. Each represents only one segment of the whole and is powered by a mathematical equation that shows how all aspects of a whole are connected. This is the first whole systems technology that shows how they all work together.

The reality is that the NTS outlines a secret method for accomplishing the seemingly impossible in business, art, science, and life. As a magician, I can keep a secret, but these secrets are too good to keep to myself. I have to share them. I never would have discovered them were it not for my interest in secrets and in accomplishing the seemingly impossible.

The magic of the NTS happens when all six of these secrets come together; when you see how each of these fit into the whole and how to use them. For me, the secrets of the NTS became clear when I saw that by following the plan of action mapped out by the symbol I was continuously connected to the points of my process that needed my attention in order for completion to be of a caliber of "top notch, astonishing, amazing results."

As a professional magician, I aim for astonishing results. I have to fine tune a process until it looks like magic. My results must surpass what my audience is used to, what high-profile business people expect, and you can create results that are just as astonishing, no matter what your business. The NTS outlines how to do so in a reliable, duplicate-able pattern.

Once you are versed in the Six Secrets of the Inner Compass and have experience with how they work, you will be able to use them to map out entire complex processes in a matter of minutes. The NTS will not only affect how you see a particular structure and cause you to solve a problem here or there, but it will help you think in a new, creative way that is in harmony with the way things are. This will help you solve numerous problems everywhere because it changes the thinking that helped create the problems in the first place. NTS thinking will help you act creatively.

The creative act is magical; it is unknowable and not completely definable. Great accomplishments often start with a vision that would have been deemed impossible only a short time before their vision became clear. This seeming impossibility is then put forth as a goal. When people believe they can accomplish a goal even though it has never been done before, suddenly it becomes possible. This has happened again and again in history. (John F. Kennedy envisioned a man on the moon. Bill Gates and Paul Allen pictured a PC on every desktop. Michael Phelps saw himself surpassing Mark Spitz's 1972 record of seven gold medals.)

The impossible becomes possible through study, experimentation, repetition, imagination and more than we can define. The NTS maps it out for us in an efficient and repeatable pattern.

> Nothing lasting manifests if you do not follow this pattern. Some people follow it without knowing it, but having this understanding gives you a great advantage.

This symbol describes, in an intriguing and practical way, how things work. It maps out how the parts connect with the whole for everything that grows in cycles (which is just about everything). It shows sustainability in action. Since each process is unique, every NTS is different, and there can't be just one way to set up your NTS that will work for every one. This is why, in this chapter, we have started with a small bit of theory, an outline of what results to look for and an introduction to the practical aspects of making an NTS.

At www.AccomplishTheImpossible.com/symbols, you can view videos about how the NTS works. This adds a visual approach to your study that is impossible to provide in the pages of a book. You can even open a free account and begin working with your own NTS. Whether your NTS is online or on paper, you will gain an advantage by reading this book.

You are about to learn a simple way to work with anything, an easy shortcut toward mastery. Most people would agree that we need to simplify the way we work in fields such as health care, transportation, waste management, public education and the legal system. With the NTS we can simplify the complexity that has grown to the point of absurdity. It will also give you a way to detect patterns within important functions. Although the NTS provides a simple way to work with any process, learning it is like learning a language, which means that effort will be involved.

The reason this information has not been more available until now is that the source of this symbol and the original material connected with it are deep, focused and complex. When the enneagram was first revealed by Gurdjieff, the focus was on human transformation, which requires far more than a single tool. To use it for process transformation, I narrowed the focus of this tool.

Once I started using it with corporate groups, I found the need to distinguish it, not from its source, but rather from subsequent interpretations unrelated to sustainability and transformation. This is why I use its full name, Nine Term Symbol (NTS), which translates *ennea* into nine and *gram* into symbol. The word *term* refers to the points. Once a symbol is labeled with the steps and inputs for a given process, we can say that the *terms* for that process have been identified. I have placed a bit of my understanding of the source and some intriguing information about the origins of this symbol into the "Acknowledgements" chapter near the end of this book. This also includes information about the origin of the Six Secrets. Although that kind of information more often comes in the form of a preface, I believe it's best to concentrate on the simple ideas that make this remarkable symbol work and save the history and the credits for later.

The NTS not only helps us solve problems, but it helps us see the structure of existence and communicate with others about the laws in operation. It turns complexity into clarity and transparency. All of these benefits and more will follow from learning the language and applying the NTS to a familiar process that matters. In the following chapters, we will look at some simple, common activities to witness how the Six Secrets work in real life. Then in chapter five, I will help you to map out and build your very own Nine Term Symbol.

CHAPTER 3

The NTS in Action

The best way to begin to understand how the NTS works is to see how it fits into the process of something you already like to do and know how to do well. Why? Because when you like to do something and are good at it, you will be successful at it again and again—and when you repeat your success, you are using the NTS, whether you realize it or not.

In a future chapter you will chart something you are good at and enjoy doing. But in this chapter I will first demonstrate how the NTS works by charting an example from my own life—snorkeling. I travel to Hawaii often, where I have a condo. I work hard all year to put on my magic shows, and when I get to Hawaii, I am tired and ready to relax. Snorkeling is the perfect activity—the glory and majesty of the underwater world restores and renews me, and inspires me to create more impressive magic shows.

As a magician, I am always thinking about the laws of physics, and it is such a wonder to be in a place where different physical laws seem to govern the world. Gravity seems to have disappeared. I have equipment that allows me to breathe where I should not be able to breathe, and I am allowed access to a world that is otherwise inaccessible. To me, this is its own kind of magic.

I have been snorkeling for years, and I'm a strong swimmer. I would not consider myself to be an "expert" snorkeler, but I am accomplished and have proven repeatedly that I am capable at it. (When you choose an activity that you do well to map out on an NTS, as you will in an upcoming chapter, you will want to use the same criteria. You don't need to be an expert at doing a certain thing, but you do need to be competent and experienced. Don't worry—everyone is with at least one thing.)

In a tropical environment such as Hawaii, I find snorkeling to be an incredible adventure—that is, if my snorkeling trip is successful. Unfortunately, there are many ways for it not to be successful. For example, if my mask fogs up and I can't see, if the waves are dangerously high, if I chose a location where I cannot get safely in and out of the water—any one of these factors can ruin my trip. So after years of snorkeling, I have figured out a system for having a safe and fun snorkeling experience. Let's take the process that I follow and map it out according to an NTS.

First let's talk about gear. Having the right gear can make or break a snorkeling trip. At first I rented gear, trying to figure out which pieces of equipment would work best. After a few trips where I spent most of my time treading water while adjusting the snorkel and spitting in the mask to prevent fog, I figured out which gear worked for me and which didn't. I bought the best mask I could afford and a bottle of defog solution, and have never had a problem with leakage or fogging since. The smaller, inexpensive flippers work best for me, and the snorkels that do not allow water to enter when I dive down are worth the extra cost.

The next step in the snorkeling process is to plan my trip and decide on a good location. Unlike my gear, this factor changes regularly. On any given day, the best locations will be determined by the patterns of waves, swells, and wind. On an hourly basis, I can tune into detailed weather reports that can help me plan where and when to go snorkeling.

Another factor in choosing a location is to find a place where I can get in and out of the water safely. Anyone who has been to the south side of the Big Island of Hawaii knows that the entry and exit points for snorkeling are the most hazardous parts of the snorkeling process. The shoreline on the Kona coast (where I have my condo) is mostly lava rocks. On the entire island, there are only a few long, sandy beaches where it is easy to get in and out of the water. The snorkeling is usually not desirable at those beaches, whereas it can be spectacular just off the lava rocks, where there are often coral reefs. However, it won't matter how breathtaking the underwater sights are if you get knocked down by a wave or if you get cut on sharp lava.

So the first few steps of a snorkeling expedition begin with several key points. I start with my gear, and then I make plans based on the conditions of the weather and the ocean, which lead to my choice of location. When I put my NTS on paper, I saw that I adjusted my gear, my plans and the location of where I chose to snorkel all in relation to one another. I had placed these three points at 1, 2 and 4: gear, plan and location. In between plan and location, I placed conditions: the conditions of the ocean, the sun, the water, and the sky. The conditions at point 3 are kinetic and always changing.

Snorkeling

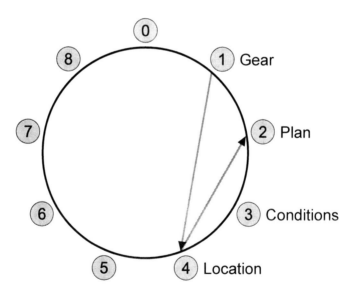

Figure 7 - Snorkeling (a)

During the trip when I used the NTS to map out my snorkeling, I saw room for improvement in my process, and those improvements followed the lines of the Compass and used the Six Secrets. The NTS was at work in the background. The improvements happened very quickly in real time:

much faster than I can describe them, and I didn't have to think about any of it. That is because my magical mind had been engaged by the NTS.

Like many beachgoers, I did not have a foolproof system for what to do with my ID, cash, and keys when I went swimming. You can't simply duct tape your keys to your ankle, and you don't want to limit your experience by swimming out only as far as you can see your stuff, your car, or your condo.

By looking at my snorkeling experience within the framework of the NTS, I willingly examined nit-picky details to streamline my process. Normally, I don't want to use my vacation time to come up with new procedures; I just want to go out and have fun. I would rather ignore small irritations than spend the time to make a change. But with my NTS in hand, I found myself making improvements quickly and efficiently.

For example, the key to my condo needed to be in a safe place. I was alone on this visit, I had only one key, and there was no central office to let me in if I lost it or locked it inside. Sometimes the front door suddenly slams shut from wind pressure, so I had to keep close track of the key. In Hawaii I'm constantly moving my key from pocket to pocket, bag to bag as I change from wet to dry clothes and take off on trips with different types of gear. On this visit, I found myself repeatedly searching for the key whenever it came time to lock the front door. This was wasting my time—time I could have been in the water. And it was embarrassing. As a magician, I want it to look like what I'm doing is what I intend. But if I get locked out, that's not what I intended, and it's not like I can just use my powers to magically appear back inside the condo like some David Copperfield trick.

When I snorkel in the ocean outside my condo, I can see my lanai and so I feel safe leaving the lanai door unlocked as a contingency if something happens to my key. But I never snorkel at only one location for an entire week. For example, just a couple of days into my vacation, the ocean didn't appear safe outside my condo because of breaking waves, and I anticipated I would walk farther south to find a safe place to go snorkeling. This is the first Secret: Anticipation.

The potential new location (4) informed my plan (2). This is the line of Communication as information about the location was being taken into account to assist the plan. Since I would be walking farther south, I had to lock all of the doors of the condo. Finally, I was motivated to change the way I was handling my one and only key.

Snorkeling

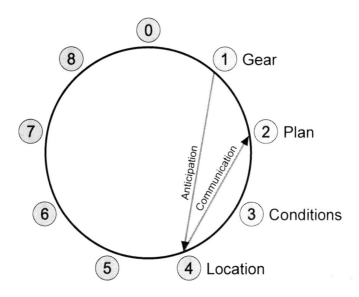

Figure 8 - Snorkeling (b) 1-4. 4-2

As I moved along the circular timeline from gear (1) to plan (2). I realized I needed to adjust my gear: to make my key more a part of the gear. So I decided to attach the key to the strap of my waterproof wallet, which solved my problem and saved time in the long run. When the strap was around my neck, I could see the key, and it was impossible to casually lose it or absent-mindedly misplace it. With this new relationship to my key, I could plan to go to any snorkeling location, lock all of the doors to my condo, and head out without fumbling through my stuff at the front door and grumbling, "Where'd I put that key?"

Of course, this change might seem trivial, but it gave me peace of mind during my excursions. I knew that my laptop and other valuables would remain safe in the condo, and that I would be able to get back inside as soon as I returned no matter how late, which made a big difference in how much I was able to relax and enjoy myself in the water.

In addition, I planned to take with me only the minimal amount of equipment required for a successful snorkeling adventure. In years past, I'd been on long hikes over lava rocks with too much gear to have an enjoyable trip, and I didn't want to repeat that experience. In anticipation of the potential location, I pared down my gear. I left many items behind that are normally part of my gear and provide comfort and convenience during snorkeling trips in hot weather. I was going to travel lightly.

Making the plan at point 2 required visualizing a stress-free experience at point 8 and responding to the conditions at point 3, as well as the information coming from the location at point 4. In Anticipation of the location, with Communication aiding my plan and through Visualization of the experience, I made choices that improved the parts affecting the whole. I visualized coming back desperately looking for my key and planned a new system making this nearly impossible. After all, I'm planning for point 8 as much as I am for the points directly in front of me. I had refined my experience (8) by making a plan (2) about how I would keep my key in sight, accessible and secure. I anticipated a snorkeling location farther away than usual. The location (4) impacted my plan (2) through the line of Communication, and I transferred my gear (1) into one lightweight backpack.

Snorkeling

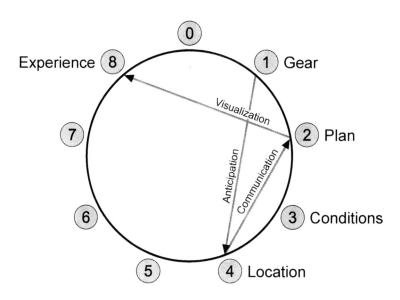

Figure 9 - Snorkeling (c) 1-4, 4-2, 2-8

I walked until I found a safe place to get in and out of the water. After viewing several options, I entered the water at a small strip of beach in between long expanses of lava rocks on either side. I knew from previous experience that this location matched the conditions as well as my fitness and skill levels, which come into play at point 6.

Snorkeling

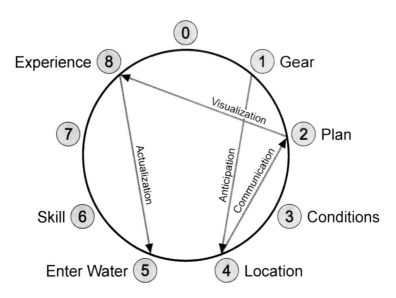

Figure 10 - Snorkeling (d) 1-4, 4-2, 2-8, 8-5

The line of Actualization is at work when the activity at point 5 (enter water) is regulated by the depth of understanding coming from the complete picture at point 8 (experience). The experience is influenced by the role of Visualization, but also through repetition. And my visualizations have depth from associations with previous experiences.

The location is refined at point 5. Actualization occurs when I enter the water at a specific location, and it brings all of my preparation into a point of no return. Once I am in the water, look down, and take a few breaths through the snorkel, Presentation begins. There are countless impressions to soak in, like the crunching sound made when a fish bites at the coral, or the delicate movement of an anemone waving like grass in a breeze. The underwater world presents its majesty: the fluorescent colors of the fish, the rippling patterns of sunlight, the silver skin of the water as seen from underneath. I earn my living by putting on shows and amazing people but when I am underwater, a show is being put on for me and I am the one being amazed.

Snorkeling

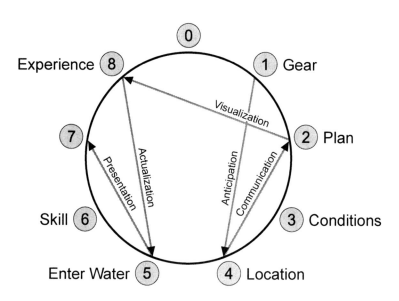

Figure 11 - Snorkeling (e) 1-4, 4-2, 2-8, 8-5, 5-7

When you enter the water you commit yourself fully to the process, and all your preparation comes into play. For example, having chosen the right mask means that the Presentation will not suffer. You are limited only by your skill (6) and the conditions (3) (which you continue to monitor). Sometimes Presentation can inspire a second wind. If you are tired, or you want to get out of the sun, but then you come upon a mother sea turtle and her baby, or some new species of bright tropical fish or coral that you have never seen before, you may start swimming with renewed energy.

The Triangle of *nature, conditions* and *skill* is the context in which snorkeling occurs. But nature is the most important of the three; it will be there long after the conditions of today and long after my skill improves or declines. Nature is the reason for the experience: the fish, the sea turtles, the coral reefs, the warming sun, and the calming undulation of the waves.

As soon as I was finished snorkeling and exited the water, I began rinsing the flippers, mask and snorkel. My equipment was expensive, and I wanted it to last. This is Restoration, which goes from point 7 (exit water) to point 1 (gear). The line of Restoration continues until I pack for the next trip because I always wash the inside of the mask with soap, which helps keep it from fogging up.

The next day there were sharks feeding outside my condo and once they were gone, there were swells, so it was still unsafe. After asking around for the best places to snorkel on other parts of the island, eventually I was told about "Two-Step," which is about thirty miles from Kona and which is named after how easy it is for snorkelers and divers to get in and out of the water there. Even in large swells, you can get in and climb out on a natural rock stairway in two easy steps. So I drove to Two-Step. Two-Step is a wonderful location that connects with a large bay, and after being in the water for a while I actually found myself snorkeling with a pod of dolphins ... a truly glorious and life-changing experience that was made possible by the NTS and its Six Secrets.

Snorkeling

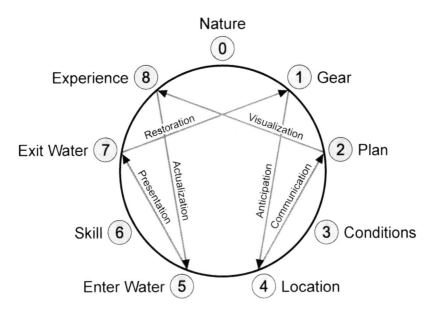

Figure 12 - Snorkeling with compass labels (full NTS)

CHAPTER 4

How a Process Can Break Down When the NTS is Not Used

In the last chapter, we discussed the magic that can happen when we use the NTS. Now, let's look at what can happen when we don't use the NTS—specifically, how a process can break down and leave you with an unsatisfactory outcome.

I am going to use as an example the experience of my friend Sam, who wanted to buy a car. The process of buying has previously been analyzed, mapped out, and described by many other writers. However, once you view the buying process within the context of the Nine Term Symbol, I believe that you will see it in a whole new way.

If you intend to buy something, you begin with a need—that is, you realize you need something. You search for a product to fulfill this need, you purchase it, and then ideally you begin to use that new item.

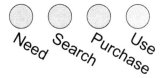

Figure 13 - Buying (a)

But is it really that simple? In a word, no, because we must add the steps of evaluating and deciding. When you purchase anything important, these two steps are crucial in the process. With this in mind, the buying process can be described as having six steps: need, search, evaluate, decide, purchase and use.

Figure 14 - Buying - Six Steps (b)

Into the gaps above we will add the factors of supply and demand, which affect every purchase to at least some extent. Supply and demand exist in an overall context of the market in which your transaction occurs.

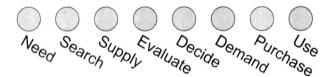

Figure 15 - Buying (c)

As a buyer, you may affect the supply and demand a tiny bit, but it affects you much more, and you cannot control it. As you search, the supply will determine what is available for you to evaluate and choose from, and the demand will affect the price.

In every process involving change or transformation, you can find at least three factors supporting the event that are independent of one another. These are the points of the Triangle in the Nine Term Symbol. In the scenario of buying something that you need, supply and demand are at the base of the Triangle, and the market is at the top, Point 0.

Buying Process

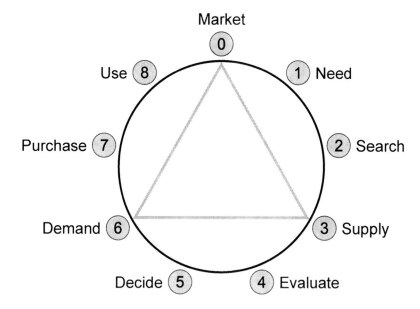

Figure 16 - Buying Process - Context Triangle (d)

Let's go back to my friend Sam, who wanted to buy a new car. A new car is a big purchase. You have probably done it yourself at least once, and therefore understand how important it is to do the necessary work required to make the right choice while avoiding paying too much. Sam certainly did the work to guarantee he would make a good choice. An artificial intelligence programmer who worked at Microsoft, he enjoyed driving his two-door red sports car but needed a larger car because his wife was expecting their first child. After doing impeccable research about what vehicle would best meet the needs of his family, Sam decided to buy a Honda wagon.

He did not like the sound system in the showroom model, and the color he wanted was not on the lot. So he arranged for a vehicle with custom sound and color to be delivered. He negotiated a good deal, and was so confident he had made the right choice that he even paid in full in advance. A week later, when his new Honda wagon was ready, he went to the dealer to pick it up. But when he walked into the showroom, he saw Honda's first SUV, the 1994 Passport, and a great display the dealer had created for it. Next to the Passport was a mountain climber's tent, and at the back of the car, rolled out on the floor, were two sleeping bags. The display was very effective, suggesting rugged outdoor fun and adventure.

Sam had an emotional reaction. He loved his wife and was excited about the baby they were going to have, but like many young fathers-to-be, he was secretly worried about losing all the fun and adventure in his life to the responsibility of parenthood. Although Sam is extremely intelligent and had chosen the wagon based on logic and information, suddenly he was being influenced by his feelings—feelings he was not even fully aware of. At this point, he started making choices without using the NTS, and the process of purchasing the car that would be best for his family started to break down. In other words, he was not using the effective, magical thinking that the NTS triggers. Before we examine how this breakdown in the process happened, let's first look at how the NTS would come into play for a successful automotive purchase.

When we hear an odd noise in the engine of our old car, or are told by a mechanic that the clutch of our car is no longer working properly, we realize the vehicle may need to be replaced. When we identify a need (for a new car), we move along the Circle Timeline of the NTS from need (1) to search (2), we begin to anticipate (1-4) how we will evaluate our potential new car.

Buying Process

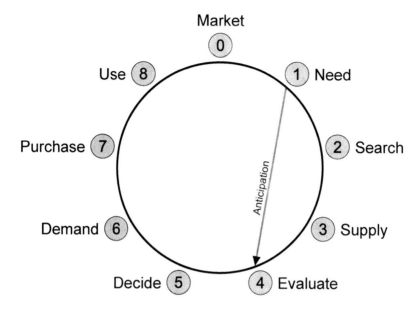

Figure 17 - Buying 1-4 (e)

There are many ways to evaluate a car. We might base our decision on repair ratings from consumer magazines, VIN records, test drives, our friends' recommendations, or a combination of these factors. Deciding how we intend to evaluate vehicles—and what we need to find—helps us focus our search.

When we have a need and we begin to think about how we are going to evaluate what it is that we need, such as a new vehicle, we are involved in the line of Anticipation (1-4). When we are evaluating and comparing, we are involved in the line of Communication (4-2). What we learn on a test drive (point 4) could be important information that will help us refine our search. For instance, at one time I was looking for more stability because my Caravan was spinning its wheels on wet pavement. During a test drive of a newer model, I learned there was an option called traction control, and I added it to my search criteria.

Buying Process

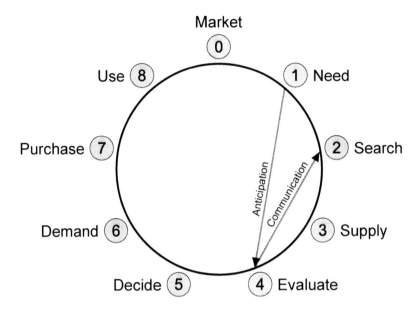

Figure 18 - Buying 1-4. 4-2 (f)

What is learned during evaluation (point 4) is communicated to the search point (2). Later, when I found myself at a gas station in an area known for heavy snow during much of the year, I saw a car in front of me that looked like the size of car that I had been looking for, but had not been on my list of potentials. I asked the owner how she liked it. She said she liked it a lot: it had traction control and it performed like four wheel drive in the snow. I was at the point of evaluation during this exchange. This impacted my search through the line of Communication. I was now determined to search for and evaluate all other models with traction control. The information you learn while you are evaluating (4) can change your entire search (2).

The next inner line goes from the search at point 2 to the use of the vehicle at point 8. This line is labeled Visualization. The more completely you visualize each specific use for your new car, the more likely you will actualize the right vehicle for your needs. The line of Actualization (8-5) depicts the action of incorporating your understanding of the end use (point 8) into the decision (point 5).

Buying Process

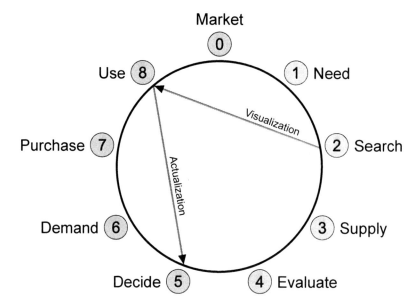

Figure 19 - Buying 2-8, 8-5 (g)

If picturing all the ways you will use your new car (Visualization) has increased your understanding of how your needs can be met, you are far more likely to make the right choice. When we bring our understanding of the end use into the critical point of no return, deciding (point 5), we are involved in Actualization. It is from here that we can steer the quality of the entire process. The Visualization begins during the search (point 2). You picture how the features you are searching for will support the activities and the interactions you want to have with your vehicle. You are visualizing how you will use the vehicle (point 8).

The line of Visualization is where my friend Sam became distracted from the process. The size and shape of the Passport appealed to Sam, and the tent and sleeping bags captured his dreams. The display hit him psychologically. Sam did not want to become domesticated, with no fast escape for quick outings. He wanted spontaneity, and to see his family life as an adventure, not a tedious routine. The display made him skip evaluation (point 4), thereby causing him to sidestep a crucial point in the process.

Convincing the dealer to let him drive home the car on display as opposed to the custom wagon took some time in the back room with a supervisor, but Sam managed it. However, once he was on the road, taking his new Passport home, he immediately discovered some problems. The sound system was less than acceptable, and although Sam knew he could install another, the car didn't handle the way he would have liked, which was something he couldn't fix. The Passport didn't feel like the right car for him.

As soon as he got home, he went online and discovered that he had made the wrong choice. Had he done some research before his impulsive buy, he would have learned that the ratings for the new Passport were far below those of the custom wagon he had previously intended to buy. The next day, Sam asked the dealer if he could return the car—but of course, the dealer said no.

In the years since this happened, Sam has come to see the magic of the Nine Term Symbol and offered to let me use this example because it shows what can happen if you either overemphasize or underemphasize one of the steps or one of the lines. Sam didn't picture the peace of mind he would feel with his newborn baby securely strapped into a safe and reliable vehicle that had gotten great ratings (Visualization: line 2-8). So, when he saw the dealer's display, he could only visualize himself in the more adventurous vehicle. If he had gone back to evaluation, point 4, he would have acquired information that would have caused him to avoid buying the wrong car (not to mention creating a serious problem for the dealership, since they had created a wagon customized to his needs). But restarting the process by going back to point 4 didn't even cross his mind—he was caught up in the moment.

If you count all of the lines, points, and labels, the Nine Term Symbol uses 25 items, supporting the idea that processes are actually complicated. A process, like the elephant in the Eastern parable, is hard to see all at once. It's not easy to find the exact place where you need to apply your attention when something unexpected happens. But once you have a feel for the Nine Term Symbol, unexpected changes can quickly be integrated into the process with precision. You simply retrace the steps and the pattern of the inner lines to find out what to attend to given the new situation. Sam should have gone backwards on his timeline to start the process all over again.

Φ◇Ђ

Continuing with the steps and secrets of the NTS as used for the buying process, we now look at Presentation and Restoration. There is a certain period in a process when what matters most is Presentation. In this case, Presentation comes just before the purchase, when the product and actual finances come together. When we connect back toward the beginning to return things to order, we are involved in Restoration.

The decision to buy something is different from the purchase itself. Online stores have many abandoned shopping carts from decisions to buy that did not turn into actual sales. At the point of the decision, the process begins to have a stronger emphasis on Presentation (5-7). When you are buying a car, Presentation may include how your credit looks, how the car looks, how the dealer acts, and what offers the dealer presents to help move you toward the purchase. Price comes into play, and so does demand. The dealer can slack off on his presentation when the demand is high because he has plenty of customers. A customer might beef up his presentation to the dealer in order to get the dealer's attention in times of high demand. Presentation comes from, and has its effect on, both parties, and it helps influence your decision.

Buying Process

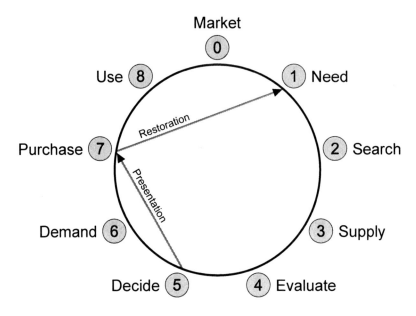

Figure 20 - Buying 5-7, 7-1 (h)

The line that connects your point of purchase back to your original need is called Restoration (7-1). Here you find yourself transferring items from your old car to your new car or into the trash. You contact your insurance agent to add the new vehicle to your policy, and you may look at ways to dispose of your old vehicle, such as putting it up for sale or donating it to charity. You may reposition the height of the hanging tennis ball you have in place in the garage to avoid bumping the wall while parking. You create files for receipts, warranties, and insurance records. Your need is met, and you reevaluate the performance of the new car in relation to your needs. Reevaluation is a form of Restoration. Sometimes, such as if you have bought a car that is totally wrong for you, Restoration/Reevaluation will send you right back into the buying process again, starting with need (step 1).

Buying Process

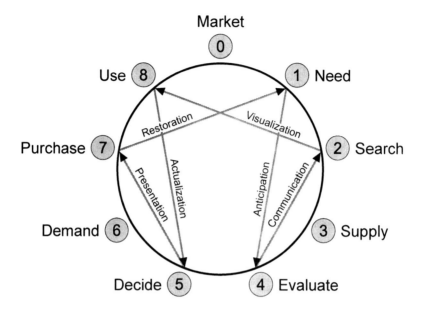

Figure 21 - Buying Process (full NTS)

We have now seen the buying process through to its completion. As we travel around the timeline of the circle, we move through it using the inner lines. The meanings of the inner lines are useful in connecting the points with the different kinds of thinking needed at each point for positive results. For example, some points, such as the evaluation (point 4) require more intellectual thinking, whereas others, such as deciding (point 5) require more emotion.

By anticipating how we will evaluate, we focus our search. Our search improves through communication coming from the field while we are actually making evaluations. By visualizing the end result, we actualize the right decision. We have seen how presentation enters to complete the purchase and how restoration begins right away as we move to point 8. Restoration brings order and completion to the end, when we can actually use the vehicle and our needs are met.

We have also seen how either trying to circumvent one step of the process or getting stuck in any one Secret can cause the whole process to be derailed. Both the deliberate purchase of the wagon and the impulse purchase of the Passport made by Sam involved every part of the Nine Term Symbol. But in each case, Sam was not aware of the Six Secrets, and how they work within a process to harmonize the whole. As a result, he ended up with a vehicle that was not really right for him. (The one consolation, he told me later, was that they treated the Passport with far less concern than if it had been the perfect car. The usual scrapes and wear and tear never bothered them, which was perfect for a young, active family.)

Sam is not the only person to be unsuccessful in a process—not by a long shot. Some people really know how to evaluate and thus spend too much time there, keeping the process from moving forward in a time-effective manner. Some immediately move from purchase back to need because what they bought cannot be used. Others cannot reach a decision or make up their minds. When a process is not flowing, it is because we do not understand all the components of the process.

The Nine Term Symbol is a catalyst between how things exist now, and how things could be in their optimal state. By applying the NTS, we learn to move through a process efficiently, and to create effective results. It keeps us from overemphasizing some parts, as Sam did. The Six Secrets are always underneath every process, and by understanding these simple secrets, we can improve the effectiveness of our results.

Can this work for our expertise? We have already seen it work in simple and quite different worlds: snorkeling and buying a car. The suspense is building. Excitement rises with the realization that there exists a secret code that we can use to understand and create important works. After all, life is a process.

The code is now spelled out in the Nine Term Symbol using the Six Secrets. As a magician, I have pledged to never reveal my secrets. These Six Secrets are different. They work in the background to guide success in processes. I can reveal these secrets without breaking the magician's code. And they are far more valuable than the tricks of my trade. By applying these secrets you can master any process, increase your knowledge, and become a magician yourself.

The Six Secrets are now out in the open; they have been revealed—at least at an introductory level. But to be absolutely sure that you understand how the NTS works on a practical level, we must now engage your understanding of it by applying the Nine Term Symbol and Six Secrets to a process you regularly use in your business or personal life. To do that, in the next chapter you'll create your very own NTS.

CHAPTER 5

Creating Your Own NTS

Now that you understand how the NTS works, it's time to create one of your own. Having your own NTS can help you refine a process, move through that process more efficiently and masterfully, and get better results. Once you have an understanding of how to use the NTS, you may want to learn more about its math, and even its ancient origins. But first, let's see how the NTS is already working in your life—whether you know it or not.

Start by choosing an activity that you are good at and that you have done at least several times with consistently successful results. Perhaps your activity comes from your work, such as providing good customer service, closing a sale, or conducting a meeting. (In my case, my activities might be booking a performance, producing an event, or successfully performing a difficult trick in front of an audience.) Or, your activity might come from your home life, such as baking a cake, playing a sonata on the piano, or rejetting your motorcycle's carburetors. If the process you have chosen is very large, such as renovating a house, you may have to break it into smaller processes, such as removing materials (tearing down) and then building up (framing, installing) and then finishing (mudding, painting, surfacing). It doesn't matter what the process is, just as long as you are experienced and competent at doing that thing. (I call this "expertise," although you don't have to be an actual expert—just someone who can do this thing competently.) And while you're at it, it might as well be something you enjoy doing—after all, this whole process of creating an NTS is supposed to be fun as well as informative.

You will be filling in the blanks to customize the NTS so that it is your very own. You'll need a sharp pencil with a good eraser, (and if you are doing it right, you are going to be glad you have a good eraser). And you will need to set aside some time to work on your symbol. The first time you create an NTS may take quite a while, but as you do it more often, you will be able to do it more quickly and efficiently.

The NTS is like a card trick. The average card trick requires you to study 15 pages of text, decipher 10 pictures and practice for several hours before you can perform it in front of someone else. But once you have mastered a card trick, it takes two minutes to perform it, and you can use it on many occasions. Similarly, once you master the NTS, you will have an entire system at your fingertips to apply to any project at any time!

The process I will choose for my NTS is:

_____

Creating Your List of Steps

Each process has definite areas where activity becomes focused before you can proceed to the next part of the process. We will refer to these "areas of activity" or "points of concentration" as "steps."

Your next task is to make a linear-style list of all the important steps of your process. Write down all of the steps involved in your process, from start to finish. Look for the most important steps that *you cannot do without*. Ideally, you want to end up with six crucial steps. But your list of steps may contain a greater or lesser number of steps. See if you can refine your list by merging some steps together or dividing some steps into more than one. You can do that now, or you can wait until you are further along with the NTS.

In the next phase, you will place the steps from your list around a blank symbol in sequential order. Your aim is to place your steps onto these six points: 1, 2, 4, 5, 7, and 8. The timeline begins at 1, and the next sequential step is at 2, and the next at 4, then 5, then 7 and 8. (We will leave out the Triangle for now: the points at 0, 3 and 6 will remain blank.)

My six chronological steps are:

1._____

2._____

4._____

5._____

7._____

8._____

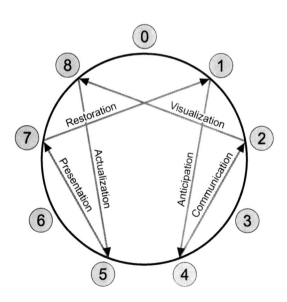

Figure 22 - NTS with space to write the six steps

As you place the steps around the NTS according to your timeline, start to consider the steps in light of the Six Secrets. At each step, two of the Six Secrets intersect, and now is the time to consider how the step relates to the Secrets, not just the chronology of your process. At this point you may want to change or refine the steps to fit the NTS. Here are some examples of questions you might ask yourself to confirm whether a step has been correctly described:

Point 1
Is the activity of step 1 something that is reevaluated, restored, or fulfilled toward the end of this process?
When at this step, will I benefit my process by anticipating the step at point 4?

Point 4
Is step 4 something that is useful to anticipate at step 1?
Does it serve the process when information about the activity involved in step 4 is communicated to step 2?

Point 2
When we are at step 4, do we communicate what is happening to step 2?
Do we tend to visualize the end result at step 8 when we are at step 2?

Point 8
What is the end result we are aiming for that we visualized at step 2?
If there is one step that we can visualize early on that will help us actualize the best result at step 5, what is it?

Point 5
What we are actualizing in step 8 (our final version of our event or creation) reaches a point of no return in step 5. What is that point of no return?
What do we have at step 5 that will be presented, served, or experienced as we move to step 7?

Point 7
What happens at the end of presentation?

What happens just before the perfect ending at point 8 and also marks the beginning of restoration or completion?

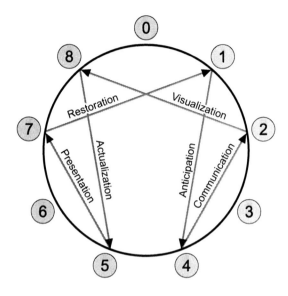

Figure 23 - NTS Blank

This movement through our process using the Six Secrets shows a pattern of connections that help us develop, improve, refine, and harmonize the steps of our process. This is the pattern experts use when they demonstrate mastery, whether by deliberate use of the NTS, or because it is their natural way of thinking. To the uninitiated, the pattern appears to represent one step after another in a chronological sequence, but actually it represents how the steps are influenced by the Six Secrets in a movement from 1 to 4 to 2 to 8 to 5 to 7 back to 1.

Labeling the Context Triangle

So far, in creating the NTS, you have not yet included the three points of the Triangle that represent forces or sources that support your process. I will call these "inputs" (to distinguish them from "steps") because without their existence and their input, the process would either fall apart or end abruptly.

The Triangle is the context in which your process occurs. Look for three vital inputs and then be ready to change them as you develop your symbol. It is most appealing to our rational mind to place these "inputs" at the points closest to when the process needs their input. But they are essentially always there and at work during the entire process.

You can now sort through the elements of your process and consider what inputs are necessary for success. These can be inputs that come from inside of us—like skill, talent, or knowledge—or they can be inputs that come from outside of us—like materials, energy, technology, or labor. The Triangle represents forces that develop over a longer period of time than the immediate process in which we are engaged. They help us create our work. Remember, these forces are present during the entire process. They may appear to enter the process at their specific point (0, 3, 6), or we may recognize that they are needed before, during, or after their sequential entry point.

You can place inputs at any of the three points of the Triangle, and you can experiment with changing or swapping various inputs at the three different points. Usually, changing these three points will not change the other six points. In other words, you can adjust the Triangle even after you have a solid sequence for the other six points. It is safe to play.

To help you find your three inputs, you can ask the following questions. Before you read the questions, keep in mind that this is not a check list. You are not trying to find an input that answers each and every question. There is great flexibility with the Triangle, and you could even apply any of the questions below to any of the three points.

Point 0
What important human desire does this process fulfill?
What is the primary reason for this activity?
What is the overarching value that holds this entire process together?

Point 3
What is the context or environment in which this process takes place?
What are the raw materials that I need for this process to happen?
What gets put into this whole system that I do not control?

Point 6
What enters into the process at about this point during the Presentation phase?
What is affected by and also contributes to this process?
What am I depending on (from others or from myself) that fits into the realm of raw materials or resources?

My points will be:

Point 0: _____

Point 3: _____

Point 6: _____

A Note About the Zero Point

The point we are calling point 0 is also point 9. Much can be said about this in a discussion of the theory of the NTS, and you can label the point 0/9, but I prefer the label "0" because, quite simply, it looks better than 0/9. Zero is the beginning, and 9 is the end. When you repeat a process, you go from 0 to 9. It is through repetition that your knowledge and experience evolve. With a successful process, the end is also the beginning of the next cycle, and you gain mastery with each repetition.

The Six Secrets

Your next task is to describe your process using the symbol and the Six Secrets: Anticipation, Communication, Visualization, Actualization, Presentation, and Restoration. When the placement of your steps around the symbol matches your understanding of your process, you have a complete and whole NTS. When it does not, you have to keep considering the steps in your process in relation to the Six Secrets until you find the right placements. In the beginning, as a visual aid, the Triangle is not shown inside the symbol because it is easy to picture the Triangle connecting its three points, and leaving it out of the diagram helps maintain focus on the Six Secrets.

When you have a working model, you have a solid start and can obtain, receive, or generate insights as you describe your process and consider your symbol. You will find some resonance with your NTS even if you are forced to recognize that it is not perfect. Even if the process of creating the NTS breaks down, you still benefit. You can see that the basics are there and that you will continue to gain more insights as you keep working at outlining your process. You can continue to consider how your sequence, as shown on your NTS, connects with the Six Secrets.

There is an art and a science to making your NTS. As you find one possible working model, hold onto it and begin working out the same process again on a blank symbol. This is one of the best ways to see more deeply into your process. Comparing one way of looking at that process with another helps you to clarify how the Six Secrets are at work.

The definitions of the Secrets come from the connections they make. It is important to see the Six Secrets at work within a process—to feel them from the inside out. This seeing and feeling will develop our ability to think with this symbol. To help us do this, we will create a list of subcategory-words to picture the full meaning of each of the Six Secrets.

Subcategory List
Anticipation
looking ahead
planning
seeing details within the heart of the activity
expanding

Communication
discussion
sharing details
sharing information
selection
concentration

Visualization
picturing
beginning with the end in mind
projection
seeing a problem as solved before the solution appears
directed imagination
comparing with an ideal
freedom

Actualization
making results happen
total quality
commitment
bringing experience into the most critical phase
creating solutions: deciphering the solution based on witnessing the problem solved
affecting or steering the quality of the product
discovering the uniqueness of a process
realization
infusing identity, clarifying the identity of the whole

Presentation
customizing
appearance
direct experience
testing, serving, regulating
framing the quality of the experience
refinement
application, utilization
interaction

Restoration
completion
finishing
reevaluation
replenishing

reorienting
recapitulation
resolving the purpose
fulfillment
integration
establishing order

Let's leave plenty of room for the above list to grow and expand. The six words: Anticipation, Communication, Visualization, Actualization, Presentation, and Restoration are labels for vital connections within processes. We call them "Six Secrets" because most people do not know about them, and understanding how they work gives you power. We can look at the six words as titles, as containers that hold qualities, or as concepts whose meanings broaden the more we consider them. As long as we recognize this, we will use the Six Secrets correctly. When you find a process that is better served by using one of the Secrets' subcategory-words from our ever-expanding list above, then use that word to define that Secret.

The NTS and Your Personal Challenges

Different people have different challenges in making an NTS, especially at first. For example, some people immediately grasp the concept of the circle, but have difficulty pinpointing the steps they take in their process. Others have an immediate, intuitive understanding of the six secrets, but cannot articulate what outside forces come into play. We all have our blind spots that we must work around—I know that I do.

I learned magic from books. Most magic books are written by magicians who are teaching their craft, and all are written for the right-handed performer. Because I am left-handed, I had to tape an "R" onto my left hand and an "L" onto my right. Many of the written descriptions of how to accomplish a magic effect are as complicated as computer programming manuals. The books on card magic are especially difficult reading, and when your hands do not match the text, learning the tricks can seem impossible. As a teenager, after hours of using a book to try to learn the most amazing tricks, I would head off to school and end my day with a driving lesson. The instructor thought he was going to die as I turned left when he said right and right when he said left. The picturing of the process of the card tricks was still going on in my mind, and it confused my sense of left and right.

So what do we do when we discover a personal weakness or challenge (like being left-handed, or not having yet grasped the concept of the circle) when we are trying to learn something new? The answer is that we keep going. Eventually I learned the card tricks, eventually I learned to drive without killing anyone, and eventually you will come to master the NTS.

The NTS of Making an NTS

Consider the steps in sequence around the timeline of your NTS. Your mind becomes aware—to some degree—of the significance of the Secrets while you progress around the circle. As you repeat a process, you will get better at the *steps*. This improving comes from the connections you make between the steps along the *inner lines*. Improvements indicate you are getting better at applying the Secrets. Continuous improvement in this system works "full circle."

Now that you have worked on your NTS, study the NTS below. The process of making your symbol can now serve as an example itself.

Making Your Symbol

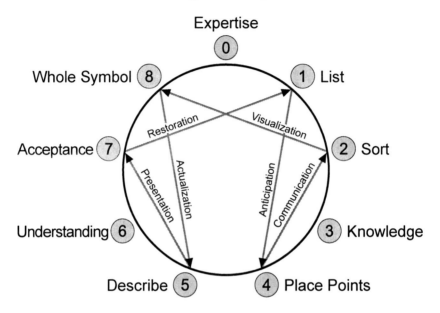

Figure 24 - Making Your Symbol

As you become proficient at applying the NTS to your processes, you will find that as you are making your list, you are anticipating where the steps will be placed on the symbol. You will notice that as you place your points, you are adjusting how you put them on the NTS due to a deeper understanding about the placements.

Your ability to visualize a whole symbol will help you actualize an accurate description of your process. When you describe your expertise, you are presenting it to your mind to find acceptance. When it works, there is an action of restoration. You put the tools away, save your files and move on to posting your symbol for future reflection. Your expertise is in front of you now in a concise, compact form that is easily accessible by your magical mind.

Call on Your NTS

Through observations you make during the repetition of your process, you will likely find ways to improve your methods along the inner lines using the Six Secrets. For example, I have seen how much time Restoration takes. I can now recognize when I am overemphasizing this line and avoiding the more difficult work (for me) of Presentation. I see the need for emphasizing one line rather than another.

You can recall and consider your NTS to find the areas that need work and to describe your observations to others. You will also be exercising your intuitive, non-linear, synthesizing mind every time you see the inner lines in action within your process. This will bring you to new understandings and a deeper level of mastery within your area of expertise.

The NTS Online

These exercises can be done online at the site dedicated to providing research for the NTS: www.AccomplishTheImpossible.com. At this website, you can create a private user name and password, and store your information so that you can make comparisons between your different symbols over time. Once you log in, there are guides for making your own NTS. You can choose whether to make your symbols available to other users, you can see examples of other users' publicly available symbols, and you can share the symbols of your choice with designated friends.

ଓ ◊ ଓ

People often vocalize their thoughts and feelings when they see me perform magic up close. I guess we tend to express ourselves when we are startled or when something out of the ordinary catches our eye. Through careful observation in these moments, I have found there are three types of basic reactions to magic.

One is of positive emotion: "I love it and I don't want to know how it's done." Another is intellectual: "I am going to think about how this was done until I figure it out." And the third is negative emotion: "I am skeptical, you can't fool me." Or: "This is frustrating; this is too hard to figure out."

People often have the same reactions to the NTS. They may love it immediately and not need to know how it works, they may intellectualize it, or they may get frustrated and feel that making an NTS is too much work. Oddly, this third reaction can be the most telling; feeling resistance to making and using an NTS may be an indicator that this is exactly what you need to do most. We'll explore this concept in the following chapters as we uncover priceless skills connected with new ways of thinking.

CHAPTER 6

The Triangle

The NTS may look a bit mysterious, but it's not a strange fad, a mystical cure, or a flashy trend. It's a system that unites disciplined thought, conscious choice, and intentional action with the forces that help you to attain completion and move toward perfection, and a crucial part of the NTS is the Context Triangle. Many universal and ancient ideas depicted in the NTS come from the Triangle.

The Triangle may seem complicated, but remember that if you're an expert at something, you're already using the principles represented by the Triangle even if you don't know it. And when you see these principles at work, you can use them more effectively to continually improve your expertise. This is possible because with the Triangle you pinpoint universal skills that can be used for all your activities.

One of the skills you develop as you use the Triangle is the ability to **see beyond the opposites** in real life situations. This comes from applying the Triangle to your thinking so that instead of seeing one force as dominating or two forces as conflicting with each other, you see three forces supporting one another and the whole. No evolution is possible when there is only conflict. When a third alternative appears, you have the Triangle.

We have talked about the Triangle in basic terms, but now let's look at it in more depth. The Triangle is both simple and complicated, and it poses a direct challenge to our normal way of thinking. We are trained to look at ideas and concepts in terms of opposites and dualities. Right versus wrong, conservative versus liberal, us versus them; this is how most of us go around viewing the world. Look at debates over political issues that make our headlines every day. We see groups with a higher degree of organization and wealth acting on groups of a lower level. We see the weak asking for help from the strong. We see one force acting upon another force, and we are taught to take sides. We are trained to accept what we like and to reject what we dislike. In general, we are wired to experience one force at a time.

But life is more complicated than this. And when we can see the world in terms more complex than simply two opposing forces, we open ourselves up to new ways of thinking—ways that inspire creativity, reconciliation, transformation, and a host of other wonderful results.

So far in this book, we have been mainly focused on the Six Secrets of the Compass because they seem familiar. They are practical and attainable. Our rational minds like to work with patterns such as the Compass, where we can list the actions we must take in an organized, step-by-step manner. The Triangle is more ethereal, and we may have to work more deeply to keep contact with the secrets represented by these three points. The Compass asks us to be dedicated to our expertise. If we keep working and fine tuning the Compass, we make progress: it is as simple as that. But the Context Triangle asks us to learn about the forces of change and transformation.

Triangles have long held a magical and mysterious place in the human consciousness. Consider the Holy Trinity, the basis of all Christian belief. Picture the pyramids of ancient Egypt, where the people buried their deified kings to send them off on their final journey. The Egyptians didn't use a cube, or a sphere like the Epcot center; they used a triangle for this divine task. It is worth repeating that in physics, triangles are known for their strength and stability because of the way they evenly distribute any force applied to their structure. And in our work with the NTS, the Triangle is a solid and effective tool that can help us learn to think beyond mere dualities.

To look at a hot-button political issue without taking sides is difficult. But when we are able to hold two opposites apart, a third can magically arise. People who are able to do this and who can see both sides of an argument at the same time and can articulate the positive elements of each are rare. Most people do not see the reconciling nature of everything, the harmonious factor, that which unites the opposites into a triangle of forces that can fuel our continuous improvement.

The Context Triangle can help you develop this way of thinking. It will guide you to put aside dualistic thinking and to look at the world in a new way. The more we see beyond polarity and the opposing forces that shape our world and our minds, the more we develop our sensitivity to a third-alternative-harmonizing-principle-force, or "third force" for short.

The Third Force

Let's consider an example of moving beyond dualistic thinking. Let's say you are doing a project with a co-worker. You are writing an article together to be published in a trade journal. You wrote a rough draft, gave it to him to review, and then you inputted his edits and comments using the "track changes" function in Microsoft Word. Unfortunately, your friend doesn't know how this works, and when he gets the document back he thinks (mistakenly) that you are taking credit for his ideas and presenting them as your own. He comes to this conclusion because every edit and comment has your name on it as the "author," and none of them appear to be his. But this was just how the computer tracked your typing. (When changes are made to a Word document, the edits and comments can be tracked and conveniently displayed in order to see the original or the changed versions. But when one typist enters in many different authors' changes, the system can only attribute the changes to that one typist.) Your co-worker believes his irritation is justified, and when he calls to complain, you cannot get a word in edgeways to explain how "track changes" works. His behavior is out of line, and you have been falsely accused.

It would be easy to look at this situation from a dualistic standpoint: you're right, and he's wrong. And if you did, you might think, "Forget it. I can't work with someone who's going to behave like this." But the article is important for yourself and for others, and you've already done so much work on it; you don't want to just throw it away. In other words, you want to reach a state of completion. In order to find the reconciling force, you hold these two opposite points of view—yours and his—at the same time, and you wait to see if a third presents itself. Now, when I say "you hold them," I do not mean that you merge them or that you blend them into compromises. I mean that you allow each to exist simultaneously and that you don't react to one over the other. Just this act alone will help you develop certain qualities in yourself that lead to a way of allowing for an opening.

Remember, you can think of the Context Triangle as evenly distributing three contributing factors to every recurring activity. The top point, the apex, represents the third force *when* it is labeled with the factor that assists with transformation and provides harmony for the two opposing forces below. Ask yourself—what could create stability in this situation? We are not looking for a graceful way to sweep a conflict under the carpet; that would neither be sustainable nor transformative. Not reacting automatically to the accusations and being able to stay calm would certainly help. It isn't easy, but if you could do it, you would be manifesting the beginnings of third force. You could then deepen your connection and find compassion for your friend; try to see his real underlying needs or fears. And maybe your co-author, seeing that you are calm, would calm down enough to listen to what you have to say. When a process goes well, it is often because we have implemented the third force unconsciously, but the Context Triangle helps us to do so consciously. In this case, you do not *become* the third force, but you carry it and bring it in to be part of your process.

ങ◊ഌ

Let's consider another example. You are an architect. Someone hires you to design a house, and takes your design and uses it, but then refuses to pay you. This is not only infuriating and illegal, but it creates a severe financial problem for you. Again, in this situation, the other person is clearly in the wrong and you are clearly in the right. But what is the third force in this situation? If you get upset enough about this injustice, you aren't going to be able to do your best work for your other clients, which in turn could cause you to lose more money at the very moment when you can't afford to.

Maybe the third force here is a handing over and letting go. You hire a good lawyer, you provide her with all the information she needs, and then you put the matter in God's hands, or the universe's hands, or at least in the hands of the American legal system. Getting away from the "I'm right and you're wrong" perspective allows you to shift your focus and creative energies to other projects. (After all, your creative energy is limited—you don't want to spend it all on anger.) Whatever allows you to shift your focus to proactive forward movement would be the third force.

There is no final answer to the question "what is third force?" because we can always learn more. There are degrees or levels of our understanding, and third force can always move deeper or ascend to a higher level. The Context Triangle guides us toward harmonizing with the agents of change and the transformations within our process. The Triangle is difficult to master because using it depends on us constantly seeing things in a new way and being creative. By working on what we can do, while having an awareness of the forces represented in the Triangle, we gradually discover our relationship to these forces and eventually learn to incorporate all three at once into our processes.

Leaders who have this understanding can assist organizational change and organizational effectiveness. Since change is constant, understanding the Triangle helps organize change according to timeless principles and core values such as inclusiveness. With this understanding, conflict is not avoided, but endured so as to invite the third force into the experience. This principle leads to greater effectiveness because it embraces the emerging changes that can power the whole system.

The Law of Three

The Triangle is a symbol that illustrates the law of three. The law of three is part of Gurdjieff's philosophy. It states that every phenomenon or process is made up of three independent forces: an active force, a receptive force, and a reconciling force. These three forces are in everything at all times, but normally people see only one or two.

Using our ordinary way of speaking, we can say that active forces are acting on passive or receptive forces. When they do, this actualizes a third force, which can be described as the reconciling force. People usually think that this reconciling force is just a product of the other two. To see this third force as independent of the others can be Earth-shattering to Western minds.

As we examine the three forces, we may use different words to describe them based on the scenario we are discussing. We have "first force" which is active, "second force," which is passive or receptive, and we have "third force," which is reconciling.

In the example of writing the article, the Triangle was your friend's active accusations (first force), you were in the passive or receptive position (second force), and your calm, compassionate, non-reactive strategy provided the time and space he needed to feel recognized so that the two of you could get back to work (third force). The creating of the article has its own Triangle: the skills of the authors (active), the important information (passive), and the market for the article (reconciling). In fact, if the market is strong enough, the thought of your article's success can help you remain calm when your co-author gets sidetracked.

Of the many sources on this subject, one of the easiest to understand is John G. Bennett. In various books of his work, he uses simple examples to outline how the three forces combine to produce different results.

A classic Bennett example of these three elements is a garden. Before the garden can exist, there is the field (the untilled land). Then a gardener comes along and turns the field into a vegetable garden. It's beautiful, and the placement of the rows, the choices of color, the timing of the plants, the fences, gates, benches and arbors have all been masterfully planned. As in many systems, the needs of each of the three elements are symbiotic: the field needs the gardener to till it, the garden needs the field as a place to be planted, and the gardener needs the garden for food.

In this example, the untilled land is passive, the gardener is active, and the garden is reconciling. To be passive is not a negative—the field is not a bad thing, although you must work to make it into something. But if you don't have the field in the first place, you won't have a garden at the end. The garden is usually seen as the result, but it has a life of its own. The garden is independent. The quality of the garden gives meaning to the other two forces. If the garden is glorious, the gardener looks good. The garden makes the gardener. In any process when the three independent forces are at work and in harmony, completion is possible. In this case, completion leads to a delicious salad on the dinner table.

ఌ ◊ ౭

So far, using real-life examples, we have been looking at hypothetical conflicts. However, there are many times when one can consider the Triangle without a conflict. For example, when I perform my shows, I am almost always active and my audience is receptive. But there are those rare times when I suddenly find myself not performing in the usual way: the way that requires my being active and using force. I do not mean brute force. I mean that there is usually a need to be a bit forceful as an entertainer. You sometimes have to talk louder than the heckler or quickly raise your hand up to cut off the applause because the audience is clapping before the final effect. You have to make things happen on schedule, in sequence, and "make it so" no matter what the circumstances.

This requires being active, or the use of the active force. But on rare occasions, the show performs itself. In this case, the show is the third force in the Context Triangle of *magician*, *audience* and *show*. The magician does not make the show. If he did, every show would be the same, like identical cookies in a cookie factory. Thank God, every show is different. How else could I have performed the same effect since I was a child without getting tired of it? How else could I have performed the same show thousands of times? I can do it because every show is different even when it is the exact same show. Why? How? It is because the *audience* is different. And just like teachers can tell you what kind of year they will have based on the feeling of a class, performers can tell you what type of show you will have based on the feeling of your audience.

And then there are those rare times when it seems like the show—the product resulting from the same old routine and the new audience—creates something incredible that exceeds all my expectations. It is impossible to accurately explain these moments of creativity in action. They go beyond mere words, and our perceptions cannot grasp these moments to explain them later. But we can have an intuition about this process. It is possible to sense that the third force—*the show*, in this case—is initiating the experience. It, rather than I, is guiding these moments. There is a sense of emptiness in action. This same type of rare experience is described by many artists who repeat their expertise and pay attention to what is happening inwardly as well as outwardly.

The Triangle can also be seen at work in the configuration of *audience*, *message* and *values*. One of my most creative show series teaches the value of sustainability. During these shows, I produce effects demonstrating Recycling, Waste Reduction, Water Preservation and other environmental sciences; and I perform these shows for students and faculty in educational settings all over the county. They have become quite popular, and after each show, as I am packing up, students ask me questions about how I do the magic. They seem to be more interested in how I made a fire ball burst out of an aluminum can than the ideas of saving energy. But when I ask them what message a particular magic effect is teaching, they explode with answers. They light up with interest, and they know exactly what the message is. You get the sense that these students want to "be the change they want to see in the world" as Gandhi said. I believe the message (my show) is active and is aimed at inspiring values (reconciling) in the audience (receptive).

The results of the value of sustainability affecting change in behavior after my show has been measured by governmental agencies. That's right, there are even metrics in magic. Several waste haulers measured how many pounds reached the landfill and how many pounds went into the recycling stream before and after my tour hit the schools in a city. Recycling went way up! I believe this is due to the value (inspired by the message) having lasting impressions in the audience.

This way of thinking is simple but not necessarily easy to practice. Understanding the Inner Compass and how to use the Six Secrets helps make the NTS quickly useable. The Triangle is even more simplistic than the Compass, but that does not make it easier. Because the points of the Triangle can change from process to process, a factor that might at one point be the carrier of the active force can later be receptive.

You can see what this is like when you observe yourself going between being active and receptive during a process. Let's say you are working at an advertising agency and have spent all day trying to brainstorm ideas. You go into a department meeting armed with what you've come up with, saying, "Hey, everyone, listen to my ideas!" But then a coworker shares her ideas, and some of them are brilliant. Then all of a sudden you stop and say, "Hey, what great ideas!" And when you do, you become receptive. Your role has shifted. You have set aside the ideas you came in with, opened your mind, and you are guiding your receptivity. This promotes creative thinking and helps everyone involved move toward completion.

People think they have to be active all the time, but sometimes what they really need to do is relax and be receptive, because being receptive can produce just as good—if not better—results than being active. The trick is to be open to taking on different roles as they come up naturally. And roles change for non-human elements, too. For example, the carrot is part of the vegetable garden, which is reconciling. When the carrot has been pulled from the ground, washed, peeled, and chopped, it becomes part of the salad, which provides active elements of nutrition to the receptive people eating it. This is what makes the Triangle both exciting and challenging— unlike the points of the Compass, the elements of the Triangle change.

Another classic Bennett example of the law of three is that of an *island*, a *mainland*, and a *bridge* that connects them. Life on the island was going at a much slower pace than life on the mainland. Then a bridge was built to connect them, and transformation happened on both sides. The island was receptive, the mainland was active, and the bridge was the source for the reconciling force. The word "source" is important because many interactions and configurations of evolution become possible through the existence of the bridge. The bridge itself is not the third force, but rather is that which allows the third force to enter the many processes that result from its existence.

This third force is commonly believed not to exist. It is invisible sometimes even to those of us whose world view includes it. The Triangle reveals that which is ordinarily hidden. But then, the magic of the NTS is that it brings both the invisible and the visible into a relationship.

As we focus on the Compass, with what is more familiar, the ideas of the Triangle will begin to make sense. To begin using the Triangle, you simply label it with the *context* of the process and consider its three points as "inputs." It is important to note that the Context Triangle can be labeled however you wish. You do not have to place the label that represents the third force at point 6 for example. And especially in the beginning, you do not have to know for sure which force is represented at each point of your Context Triangle. The deeper ideas represented by the Triangle like the three forces and how they interact will grow on you. This is what makes the NTS fun and compelling: it provides a form for your mind to work with magical ideas that lead you to greater understanding.

On a side note, the lines of the Triangle indicate that the three forces belong together or that they originate from an unknowable unity. These lines can not have labels like the Compass. The points of the Triangle would be the only spot to put a label such as "first, second or third force," but not along the lines of the Triangle. We do not usually place any such label at those three points because the forces are flexible. We simply label the three points of the Triangle with the "functional inputs" required for the process. As you work with the Triangle, you will recognize which point represents first force, which point is acting as second force and which is representing the third force. If needed, you can label the three forces with a plus sign for first force (active), a minus sign for second force (receptive or passive), and an equal sign for third force (reconciling or equalizing). For those working in this way, it is important to remain open to the flexibility inherent in the Law of Three.

In working with the NTS at any level in any capacity, we bring our consciousness to the pattern that involves third force. It's not about doing away with opposing forces nor is it about setting them up to devour each other. This pattern points to a balance between opposites where the balance does not make the opposites go away but becomes a third principle. Working with a pattern that allows for the existence of the third force is an unusual but necessary practice if we are to reconcile the forces at play in this magical world. This gives us the power to create. Then, when we apply the various techniques that are supposed to make changes happen, we will succeed because we are working with more than opposing forces. We are working with creativity in action.

CHAPTER 7

Beyond Illusion

I have given presentations on how to make an NTS to countless groups of people, and I am always surprised by the resistance some people feel in actually doing it. (Interestingly, it is often those who resist the most who end up getting the most out of it.) You, as a reader, may be feeling some resistance too, and wonder if the effort of making your own NTS is worth the benefits. One benefit, of course, is to experience wonder. But is wonder enough? In his famous quote, Einstein said that wonder is critical to art and science, "The most beautiful thing we can experience is the mysterious. It is the source of all true art and all science. He to whom this emotion is a stranger, who can no longer pause to wonder and stand rapt in awe, is as good as dead: his eyes are closed."

People imagine they can change something within themselves (such as having the ability to "think outside the box") just by knowing about the subject. This is an illusion; change requires a growth in understanding. Real understanding comes only as knowledge enters into practical experience. For this people must make efforts; they must consciously call upon their attention to use their knowledge in real situations.

This is sometimes called "practice." In the performing arts, it is called "rehearsal." Normally you do not rehearse in front of an audience. But as every expert in the performing arts knows, the more you perform in front of live audiences, the better you get. Practice and rehearsal lead to experience and understanding. One must experience one's understanding in action over and over to progress. Repetition with conscious attention leads to growth in understanding. This gives one the power to change.

A higher level of understanding leads to greater creativity. Creativity is mysterious and unpredictable. As creativity enters into a process, it brings with it the power to change the whole. Finding ways to keep creativity alive is of the utmost importance for success. Performing astonishing results takes hard work, constant attention, and effort, but at some point, creativity, ingenuity, and grace will enter to aid the efforts. We can use some help establishing patterns that aid our connection to creative thinking and to working with our Right Brain.

Businesses have used my magic shows to make lasting impressions of quality and the emotional impact of astonishment on their employees and clients. To this end I have attended numerous meetings with various clients at which someone on the event team indicated that they needed to get their audience to think outside the box—that is, to engage in new and creative ways of problem solving. I always wonder, why do they think they need this? Have they ever met someone who can actually think outside the box? Have they seen him or her achieve success because of it?

Just because we know the phrase "think outside the box" in no way implies we know how to do it or can do it at will. This is not an automatic ability that can be turned on by anyone with the mere flick of a switch. But it is necessary. Companies hire magicians like me to inspire people to think outside of the box. Magic is great for this, since it reminds us that the world in which we live is magnificent and mysterious and that we do not know everything. It reminds us that there are laws at play that we do not see while at the same time it seeks to inspire wonder and astonishment.

In business, we need these reminders because we function in environments where salaries are paid to those who appear to know things. The more things you appear to know, the more you seem to deserve your position and the more you will get paid. You can't rise to the top in a business by being in a constant state of awe and by admitting the limitations of your knowledge and by only asking questions. But we need more of this—we need to be comfortable with the unknowable, because it is what drives true creativity. This is exactly what we need to discover new ideas and to think "outside the box."

Albert Einstein said, "I am enough of an artist to draw freely upon my imagination. Imagination is more important than knowledge. Knowledge is limited. Imagination encircles the world."

Einstein understood that creative thought is unique and connects with the right use of our imagination. In this regard, **business can learn from the arts**.

The Nine Term Symbol integrates creative and logical thinking. It asks us to view our work in a new way. It is worth repeating that the NTS creatively encourages our attention to see the whole while simultaneously connecting the parts in new ways along proven lines of success. Once you have your first NTS in front of you, put it up on a board and refer to it regularly. It will grow on you and reward you with views outside the box.

Ideas provide energy. In physics, the most basic definition of energy is something that has an action. If something has an action on us (that is, it motivates us to act), it has energy. The NTS gives us energy in that it has an action on us when we know how to use it. The energy given to us can be described as new ways of thinking, or as intuitive connections at work on a subconscious level.

Carl Jung's book *Man and His Symbols* was written to give us an understanding of the importance of our subconscious mind and ways to relate with it. Many of us think linearly and do not have the tools to intentionally connect with our unconscious mind in order to harness its power. The Nine Term Symbol provides the form and sequence for the Left Brain to map out a process using the rational mind while simultaneously allowing the Right Brain to engage with the same process from its equally relevant, non-linear point of view using the creative (or magical) mind.

If you are not feeling excited about what I am saying, your work here may be finished. You can close this book now. However, what if along with your ambivalence there is a realization that you are not operating as effectively as you could be? A feeling of ambivalence may be masking a desire for improvement—we care about the ultimate impact we make in the world. We can admit that we do not know how to flick on the switch of creativity. It was not that difficult to develop your very own NTS of a familiar process. You see there is something true in this symbol; it can be used to describe any expertise. Your first NTS may seem incomplete, or, on the other hand, it may look like a perfect representation of your activity.

In either case, your NTS will develop as you engage your mind with the ideas contained in the symbol. When you go through your process again and again (repetition) using this symbol, your understanding will grow.

Developing our understanding leads us to new ways of thinking. And that is a huge mental benefit of working with the NTS. But it's not the only one. There is a constant need to pay attention when performing magic (the art of producing astonishing results). As soon as one step is completed, the next step must be prepared for. To prepare for the next step, attention must be paid in advance to what this next step requires. This inevitably requires divided attention.

These days, attention is at a premium. People do not know how to develop, work with, or even simply recognize their attention. No wonder creativity and ingenuity are valued now more than ever, because they are in such short supply. In this rapidly-changing, technology-based world, there are constant requests for and even attacks on your attention. If you have not refined your attention skills, how are you going to divide your attention or even focus it in one place for any duration? Making and using an NTS will help you develop and refine your attention. It trains you in the discipline of sustaining your attention from start to finish—to a point of completion. These are priceless skills for someone wanting to achieve astonishing results, no matter what your field.

The NTS and Creative Thinking

As a planet, we are in desperate need of new ways of thinking because the old ways just aren't working. If they were, we wouldn't have war, we wouldn't be ruining the environment, and people wouldn't be dying of hunger. But we keep carrying on with the same old way of thinking. And as Albert Einstein said, "We can't solve problems by using the same kind of thinking we used when we created them." The NTS can help us to develop new ways of thinking and to see life in new ways—and so can magic.

I once went to a dinner party where the hostess, my client Gretchen, had asked me to do some tricks without revealing to the other guests that I was a magician. (This would normally be against my ethics, but I decided to go ahead with the charade and then decide later in the evening whether or not to reveal my true identity.) So I told everyone that I worked in real estate. After dinner was served, I mentioned to the guests that I had had a lot of strange experiences as a child. When they asked me for examples, I said that I used to be able to blow bubbles and then make them freeze in the air with my mind.

"Do you think you could still do it?" asked Gretchen, who of course knew what was really going on.

"I don't know," I responded. "Shall I try and see? Do you have any soap?" And she went into the kitchen and got soap—a special soap that I had planted there earlier. I took a straw, blew some bubbles, and then suspended the bubbles, motionless, in midair. The other dinner guests could not believe their eyes, and there was a shocked silence around the table.

I said that wasn't the only thing I was able to do as a child. As the meal went on I "borrowed" objects like playing cards that were shuffled endlessly and yet matched the order of another deck in a drawer in Gretchen's library, books that were opened to random pages on which I knew the exact words without looking, and numbers chosen by the guests and written on a pad of paper sitting by the telephone that totaled the same number I had written on a slip of paper and handed to one of the guests a few moments before.

A powerful feeling of mystery and the clear sense that anything is possible was palpable among the other guests. You could sense it in the air and in their breathing, which had become slower and more deliberate. Normally, I am a magician pretending to do the impossible in order to amaze and enchant my audience who all know that I am using tricks and skills. They suspend their disbelief. In this occasion, I was using the tricks and skills while pretending *not* to be a magician. This difference created an eerie sense of awe in my audience that night. They were not willingly suspending their disbelief; it was challenged to the core.

Three of the guests in particular interested me. One was a senior gentleman. It was clear to me from his expensive suit and his manner of speaking and of comporting himself that he was a man of means who had done well professionally. The other two were a young couple who had become engaged rather quickly after meeting. The young woman was gorgeous; the young man was up and coming in the business world.

As a magician, I am used to applause after a trick, but there was no applause here—only incredulous questions like, "Are you kidding me?" and "Have you ever tried to use this to win the lottery?" In general, the guests just seemed gutted with disbelief. Meanwhile, the young engaged woman seated to my left and her fiancé on my right seemed to gradually discover that they had differing views about the unknowable. She accepted everything as though it were natural and beautiful and just wanted to enjoy it while he was busy trying to come up with a logical explanation because it challenged everything he thought he knew, and so he needed to explain it. They almost got into an argument about it. I thought about the fact that they had not known each other long before getting engaged, and it seemed to me that coming up against something they could not explain was highlighting their differences to each other.

As for the older gentleman, he looked utterly shocked by what he was witnessing. He was pale and looked like he had just gone through a harrowing near-death experience, as if he was realizing for the first time that after all these years of thinking he knew what life was all about, maybe he had been utterly wrong. His beliefs about reality had been shaken to the core, or at least that's what I saw when I looked in his eyes.

Just then, our hostess, Gretchen, came out of the kitchen and said that something terrible had happened—the cake that she had made for dessert had not come out properly and was ruined. She asked me, "Can you do something to make it right?" That was my cue to perform a classic of magic called "baking a cake." I was sure it would solve my ethical dilemma of revealing my identity, since this particular trick would be a dead give-a-way that I was a magician, like pulling a rabbit out of a hat. I fully expected everyone would realize what had been going on.

I asked Gretchen for a pan and some flour. "Oh, and bring us a couple of eggs while you're at it," I said. I tossed the flour into the pan, cracked the eggs and was careful to remove the shells.

"Now, if we put a little bit of your failed dessert into the mix..." Gretchen grabbed a handful of her half-baked cake. I pointed to the pan. She tossed it in. I asked for some chocolate and some lighter fluid, and a match. She had them all within reach (no one questioned why she had all these items close at hand). I lit the glop in the pan on fire and began to circulate the pan above the table in a magical ritualistic style. The fire was hot and rising up to the chandelier when I grabbed the cake pan's top to cover the fire to put it out. I lowered the pan to eyelevel and pulled off the top with a gesture like a fancy waiter. Inside the pan, the glop was gone and in its place was a fine chocolate cake that Gretchen had baked the night before. I was astonished when, instead of realizing that I was a magician, the guests seemed to be even more convinced that I was some kind of savant with miraculous powers! The people around the table were so staggered by my display that they almost could not regain their composure.

After dinner, the senior gentleman approached me. I could see that his normal way of thinking (reality-based thinking, where he only believed what he saw with his own eyes) had been challenged. I had a sense that the evening had made him look at his life in a different way, that it had opened up a world of possibilities, that now he might try things he had never tried before.

He said to me, "I know you're not a real estate broker; I know something was going on here. I can't say what it was, but whatever it was you really opened my eyes tonight." It was kind of a gentleman's acknowledgment, a tipping of his hat to me, and I accepted his compliment without feeling that I needed to reveal my true vocation.

If I had one wish for this man it would be the same wish I have for everyone: that they understand they can do anything they want to do, and that sometimes we have to attempt to do the impossible to find out what is actually possible.

As we all said goodbye to our hostess I wondered if the young couple would indeed marry because they seemed so different from each other. I later heard from Gretchen that they didn't end up getting married. While I would hate to think that my performance broke up a relationship (and I am sure there were many other factors) we show much about our true selves by how we react when we are faced with a new way of thinking. If the two young people were not suited to each other (as evidenced by their wildly different reactions to what they were seeing) then I suppose it was better for them to find that out sooner rather than later.

On the way home from the dinner party, when I was finally alone in my car with all my props, I experienced tears. I was moved by the sheer immensity of this art, of "my" art, in which I am just a small practitioner.

Whereas after a show I normally reflect on how well I performed or what I could improve upon, after this dinner party, I connected firsthand with the overwhelming power of the art of magic. I realized how noble my profession is and that my role as a magician is a real and sacred responsibility—one I will always value more after having this experience, which perhaps amazed me more than it did my audience.

I now realize that we changed the Triangle at this event. Magic shows normally have a Triangle of *magician, audience* and *entertainment* where entertainment is the purpose and is achieved through wonder, astonishment and awe. Since the audience did not know that the demonstrations were just for their entertainment, there was a tension in the air. We changed *the purpose*, which is one of the points on the Triangle. We took away the audience's knowledge of *the purpose*, which created more tension because the third force had to be found by each dinner guest on his or her own. There was no easy place to stop and say, "Oh, I know it's a trick—but still, how does he do it?"

When confronted with the impossible, our minds search for an answer; a meaningful questioning occurs in us. When given the answer, even a partial or simple answer like, "Oh, he's a magician" or "He's an entertainer," the search for understanding ceases.

Because the Triangle always brings an alternative to the necessary opposing forces, it helps us keep questions alive in life. That fuels the growth of understanding through an attitude of wonder. That fuels creativity. When knowing comes, it brings with it a reactive attitude that shuts down true questioning.

The difference between the magic I did that night and the NTS is that one is a trick and one is not. But both can make people open their minds to new possibilities and new ways of thinking, and both can trigger profound inner experiences that cause you to see the world in new ways.

CHAPTER 8

Everyday Business

New Understanding

Flexibility helps us connect a process to a form and helps our mind find the form for a sequence. While looking at any process, I like to have two versions of the NTS available: one with and one without the labels on the Compass. The absence of labels helps my mind work intuitively.

Remember our ever expanding list of words under each of the Six Secrets (page 58)? The Nine Term Symbol helps us to describe exact and specific processes by allowing for flexibility within a process. When looking at a process with the unlabeled Compass (Figure 5, page 21), the mind tends to see the connections made by the Inner Compass for what they are. Without the labels, with no words, you will sense the connections. The version of the symbol that includes the labels on the Compass is also important to have available (Figure 6, page 22). It is especially important when considering a full description of a process.

The six words that represent the Six Secrets are "title words," and the specific connection that each of the Six Secrets makes within any given process may be described by using the title word itself, by using a related word or a synonym of the title word from our ever expanding list, or by using intuition. We must be flexible.

As we know, there is motion in this symbol; it's moving in a circle and it's moving along the lines of the Inner Compass (1-4-2-8-5-7-1...). Since the symbol depicts contrasting movements within a process, the labels on the Inner Compass help us identify the Six Secrets while keeping the points and the movement along the Circle Timeline in mind. Connecting with the qualities represented by the Six Secrets enables us to make specific, quality-oriented choices while in the midst of our busy movement from point to point.

Wanting to understand an important process more deeply is an impulse worth cultivating. As your understanding grows, and you see the whole pattern of your expertise, you do not come to a fixed stopping point. With the NTS, you remain flexible and continue learning. The symbol helps you keep questions alive. As the inquiring mind holds a question, observations lead to seeing the big picture. Keeping a question alive about a process—throughout the process—expands the understanding mind. Answers come, and so does verification; this is good. But answers are not the end result. We benefit equally, if not more, from the questions themselves, from maintaining a position of not knowing all the answers and from a willingness to be amazed.

The ability to image the whole pattern of a process leads to a special kind of intentional repetition. Repetition—along with picturing the whole and striving for understanding—increases the quality of the endeavor. When you are passionate about a process this happens quite naturally. This increasing of quality is really an act of giving. You give to a process when you contribute intentionally. You are not just blindly going through the motions.

Other people involved benefit when the quality of your process improves. This resonates with an act of love: a giving that arises from a deeper understanding and flows to those who participate in the process. The NTS guides us toward intentional repetition. It gives us a pattern for increasing our understanding. With it we can find answers and make creative improvements. With the NTS, the simple striving to understand can lead us forward—in the spirit of giving—to accomplish anything we aim for, even the seemingly impossible.

Quick Views

Before you use this system to amaze your friends and astonish your co-workers, you will be able to look at several symbols created from different points of view and see into the inner working of those symbols with some clarity. It is therefore useful to look at a variety of processes to see the power of the NTS at work. Notice it describes each activity while it simultaneously provides a solid framework for finding improvements, sharing understanding, and gaining insight.

We will describe the processes below with fewer words than we used for snorkeling and buying a car. This is because we have a picture that is worth a thousand words: the NTS. So, we can already use fewer words. And as we continue to comprehend this picture—that is worth so many words—into the chapters ahead, we will continue to consolidate our descriptions. Eventually you will be able to read in detail about a process by reading the labels on the symbol and picturing the expertise.

When an expert describes her work using the NTS, those who can read the symbol will quickly see what it would be like to experience the structure of her activity. But her activity is not static; it is in motion. Everything that grows is both becoming and existing as an independent entity. The Nine Term Symbol is understood fully when you see it describing the motion of being and becoming. Remember that point "0" is also point "9," and that the processes we are involved with are evolving. The NTS is like a spiral in the sense that with every repetition, a process "becomes" and therefore spirals into new territory.

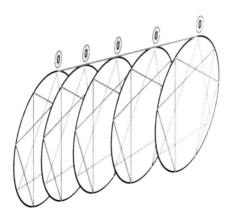

While this symbol gives you a quick view and authentic taste of another's expertise, it does not make you an instant expert in unfamiliar territory. However, using the NTS, you can see similarities and patterns that transfer from your world to another. This will help you bridge many gaps that appear impossible to cross, like those encountered in the lands of customer service.

Customer Service

As consumers, we experience everything from outstanding to lousy customer service. Most of us have filled out at least one evaluation form either in person, online, or by mail. We have a sense of how those in service roles should treat a customer, and when we are the customer, we hope for a good experience. On a regular basis, everyone relates to the service process either as a customer, provider, or both. We all participate in the customer experience. From the perspective of someone providing a service, here is the linear flow of events, the timeline.

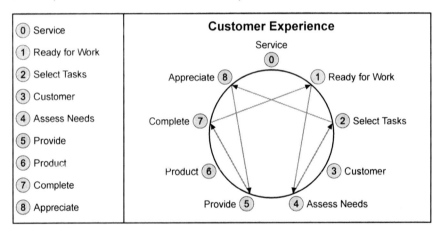

Figure 25 - Customer Experience - list & NTS

- The service person begins at point 1, ready for work, and will repeatedly return to the place of being ready after completing (7) each encounter with a customer.

- Most jobs require the selection of tasks (2) based on the flow of customers. When it is slow, there are specific types of jobs to be performed, and when traffic increases, the focus of the customer service professional remains with the customer.

- Assessing the needs of the customer (4) is an art, and the assessment affects what is provided (5) to the customer by the service person. The art of connecting with customers is an example of an inexactitude. Every process has them. Companies put effort into training their employees how to interact with customers, but there is no exact method that works for every situation. There is always a personal element that is more art than science.

- The product (6) supplied by the company enters the picture; the hope is that it will satisfy the customer's need. The service professional brings the customer (3) and the company's products and services (6) together.

- The service person must make an effort to complete (7) the interaction. This will vary according to the how effectively the inputs at 3 and 6 unite.

- The service is completed (7), and when everything goes perfectly, appreciation (8) is expressed all the way around. The customer appreciates the product, the service person, and the company, while the service person appreciates the customer.

> The description above is focused on the Circle Timeline. Figure 26 on page 89 shows the same NTS with the addition of the labels on the Compass. While reading the description that follows, focus on the Six Secrets.

Companies that value their human resources provide ways for their service folks to restore their energy and attitude in between encounters with customers (line 7-1, <u>Restoration</u>). Great customer service people can let go of the last experience and take on a new customer with a fresh approach; they get ready for work again and again throughout their shift. Great companies consider this need and cater to it.

A service person, let's call him Joe, develops the art of <u>anticipating</u> the needs of the customer (<u>1-4</u>) and keeps the aim of appreciation in mind during every task (<u>2-8</u>), even when he must leave his favorite task to attend to his least favorite. For instance, when the floor needs to be mopped in the restroom, it is for a reason that Joe cares about: customers appreciate cleanliness. On the other hand, Joe wishes to be appreciated by the customer and can <u>visualize</u> (2-8) this appreciation as an aid to selecting and accepting the most applicable tasks.

In my case, in home improvement stores, I expect to go back several times to see Joe. I often end up in a long return line with the wrong product after spending my time and money trying to figure out why it does not function the way Joe said it would. Getting to the point where Joe provides the perfect match for my needs the first time seems like an impossible fantasy. Since we are fantasizing, let us imagine Joe has read this book and boned up on the NTS.

- At point 2, Joe selects tasks that are in response to <u>anticipating</u> my needs from the future point 4. Is Joe outside of time? Not really, but before and during his move from point 1 to point 2, he must anticipate my needs.

- Through <u>visualization</u> of a great final result and attempts to complete this circle many times in the past (repetition), Joe comes to a place of being ahead of my needs in the present. This is partly how Joe will find solutions that <u>anticipate</u> my needs before his in-depth assessment happens at point 4.

- While repeating the process, Joe compares what is happening at point 4 with what is selected at point 2. This comparison involves <u>communication</u>. The communication connects point 4 with point 2 in a loop while the timeline is moving forward.

- Through <u>Anticipation</u> (1-4) and <u>Communication</u> (4-2), Joe clarifies my needs and the tasks required to fulfill those needs.

- Joe has to repeatedly arrive at point 5 (provide) and see where he and others have failed to <u>Anticipate</u>, <u>Communicate</u> and <u>Visualize</u>. Through repetition, Joe learns how to use the line of <u>Actualization</u> to deliver the quality that will amaze even an accomplished magician.

- To provide the highest quality product with the perfect blend of options for me, Joe must know (<u>visualize</u>, 2-8) what the end will be. This helps Joe with the line of <u>Actualization</u> (8-5).

- The line of <u>Actualization</u> (8-5) brings the end result into the present moment of choice. This can only be accomplished when Joe is an experienced professional who <u>anticipates</u> (1-4) my needs, and <u>communicates</u> (4-2) the important details that will help select (2) the right ingredients for a truly satisfying experience (8). This process of assessing needs and selecting tasks will be repeated until Joe selects the right set of tasks to provide (5) for my needs. The line of <u>communication</u> (4-2) is what sets up this loop.

Customer Experience

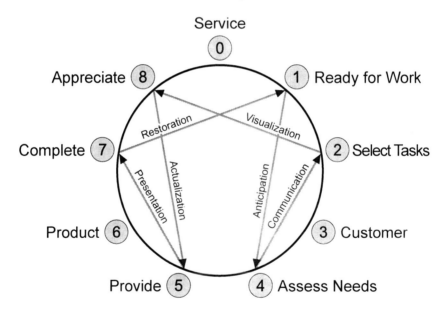

Figure 26 - Customer Experience NTS

- Then Joe provides (5) the company's products in a way that meets my needs (<u>Presentation</u>, 5-7). This leads to a sale, and if he is on commission, Joe wants me to use and not to return the items I have purchased.

- Joe presents the company's products, and when the service has been completed (7), the line of <u>Restoration</u> begins (7-1).

- The company also involves itself in the line of <u>Restoration</u> because at the moment when a service is complete (7), the product must be replenished. The shelves need restocking.

- A brief rest in the break room can do wonders to prepare for the next encounter. Customers are demanding and so is the role of service. The company relies on the service professional, as does the customer. In a successful business there is pressure on Joe to perform, and he must recover from the resulting high-tension experiences.

Being a customer or serving customers is one experience to which we all can relate. The Customer Experience is described here as though it were ideal. Should a process break down, this symbol reveals to you where the system is failing. For example, when greed usurps the value of service, systems fail to reach an honest point of completion. This can remain hidden until a major collapse or it can slowly break down the company.

Take this NTS with you when you go to a store where you really need service. It is interesting to go through a Customer Experience event with this symbol in hand to trace each connection.

Recent studies in neuroscience provide strong support for the idea that working with attention stimulates brain cells for increased learning. The Compass reveals hidden knowledge within a process. It shows you where to place your attention and helps you to divide your attention between the relevant parts and the whole. Attention is either directed or haphazard, and there are degrees in between. By directing your attention into your process intentionally rather than haphazardly, you invite creativity and increase your aptitudes in countless ways. As you apply the understanding outlined by the NTS to your personal experiences, you make new neural connections in your brain, and develop your capacities.

Sales: Getting New Customers

How do we actively get new customers? This is not a trick question. Nothing could be simpler. We find them through research, and then we work to earn them.

A sales person has a goal. He targets an attainable sales figure over a three-month period, and aims for a yearly figure as well. He researches his field of potential customers to find ones whose needs align with his company's products. He proposes a solution for his customers' needs and asks them for their business. This is often referred to as "the ask." Next, he closes the sale, which may entail having to give answers to any questions or objections. He works after closing to retain the customers for future sales.

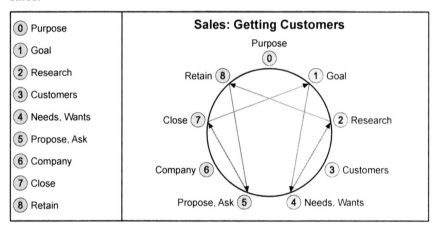

Figure 27 - Sales - list & NTS

Elizabeth is an experienced sales person. She works for a national bank that must offer personal service to retain customers. She is the reason many of her customers do not switch to a local, "more friendly" bank. But she cannot maintain her position just by serving existing clients. Elizabeth needs more customers, and the bank sets yearly quotas for her to achieve.

Elizabeth must seek out and meet potential customers. She would like to ask relevant and targeted questions of her potential customers based on previous research incorporating the needs of those customers.

A sales goal (1) challenges Elizabeth to perform. Her experience has taught her to understand her customers' needs and desires (4) before connecting them with the features of her company's products (5). Her research (2) may include understanding how a potential customer will use a product and how the product actually functions to provide a business solution. Research may be aimed only at knowing the individual customer's business, or it might go as far as finding assets on public record.

When a new need arises (4), Elizabeth must be able to incorporate the information about that need into her research. When a customer has a new need, she pays attention. Perhaps the need will become a trend and open up a whole new category of potential customers in her field. Through understanding what it takes to retain a customer (8), Elizabeth will direct her focus on solutions that clients need. The proposal (5) will then provide a client with what he needs.

Elizabeth sees the difference between offering a product with features that her customers must match to their needs, and offering usage scenarios that already fit her customers' needs and their business. Offering a usage scenario will likely close (7) the sale.

If you had to take over for Elizabeth while she goes on vacation, you could effectively use the Six Secrets, which have turned into understandable aspects inherent in processes of all kinds. Here is what you would do:

- You are looking for new customers. You have a goal.

- Before you research, you anticipate (1-4) the needs of your customers. You must know what to look for, and what they need or want.

- Your research is refined by taking into account details you learn at point 4. Through the line of communication you home in on what clients actually need.

- As you research, you visualize (2-8) retaining your clients.

- The more you know about the details involved with retaining a customer, the more likely it will be that you can address the customer's real needs (actualization, 8-5) and propose (5) an accurate scenario.

- When "the ask" is in full force, your presentation (5-7) must be aimed at closing the sale. You must account for every factor and find an answer to every question.

- As you close the sale, the act of bringing things back into order begins (7-1) and you look at the effect on your goal (1). Here you can reassess the time it took, the approach, and the strategy for the next encounter.

Sales: Getting Customers

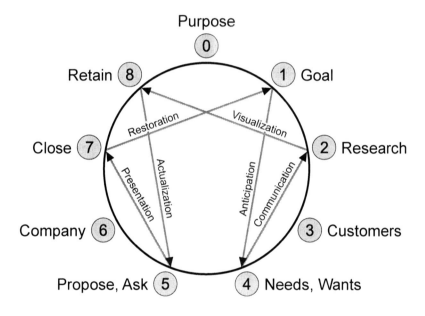

Figure 28 - Sales NTS

Everything works together in this model to bring you closer to perfection with each repetition. The key to progress is repetition, but with the Six Secrets as your Compass, the repetition remains fresh, powered with a directed attention to what matters. This produces an upgrading of quality along with the capacity to remain action oriented around the needs of the process.

System Upgrade

This NTS shows a computer system upgrade that is likely in your world, so its specifics should come in handy for you personally. For some, computer upgrading is an ongoing process. And for some, it overlaps with the Customer Experience NTS, especially when services are needed to create a successful computer system upgrade.

You have perhaps done this many times by now, and suspect the ongoing process is here to stay. Progress seems to make system upgrades unavoidable.

- Efficiency is the goal, the over-arching aim driving the entire endeavor.

- You begin finding new needs in your business and with your current system.

- Some of these needs relate to the outside world—for instance, your system and your web browser cannot keep up with the features and benefits offered at the web-sites you need for your work. You must update your browser, and eventually, your system requires an upgrade too.

(0) Efficiency

(1) Current System

(2) New Needs

(3) Technology

(4) Prepare System

(5) Modify System

(6) Our Business

(7) Use System

(8) Perfect System

Figure 29 - Upgrade list

- Astonishing amounts of money are spent on upgrades for greater efficiency in businesses today. For an upgrade to improve connections within a company's system, a deep and thorough understanding of the *business*, the user's need for *efficiency* and *technology* must be harmonized.

The tasks of the upgrade become familiar to everyone in business. I know realtors, past the age at which many retire, who are learning how to use their fourth system in ten years. They wonder about important files left on the old computers, but they cannot network the new and old machines without a major effort involving a steep learning curve.

System Upgrade

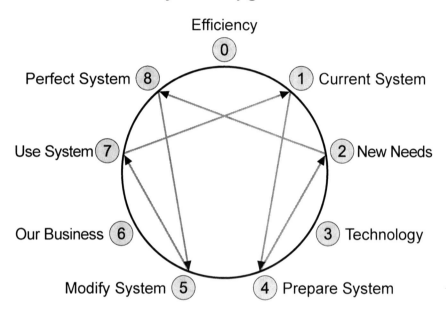

Figure 30 - Upgrade NTS (without Compass labels)

Even for low-tech, budget-conscious people, new needs arise (2) and technology (3) often has the answer. If the answer is partial, research and development come into action; otherwise, the process proceeds to the preparation (4) of the new system.

At the point when modifications (5) occur, people need to learn what's new before they begin using the new system. As they are using it, changes will be needed to perfect the system (8).

Every single point of the Compass—beyond point 2—refers to the new system. When the NTS containing the labels on the Compass is viewed, our minds can easily recognize the need for the connections emphasized by the Six Secrets (Figure 31).

Picture a modern scenario. Judy, a realtor, has hired Jason for an upgrade. Jason is working on a contract with the real estate company through which Judy is licensed. She is willing to let Jason decide what is required for her system.

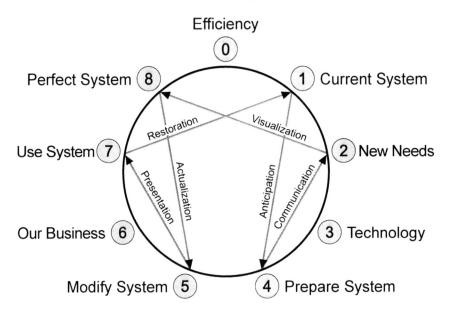

Figure 31 - Upgrade NTS

- Jason learns what Judy has in her home office (1) and <u>anticipates</u> the preparation phase (4) before deciding on the final list of new needs (2). This allows for questions about what technology is available: what is easily possible.

- Jason compares what is possible using existing technology (3) with the needs at point 2. This comparison involves the lines of <u>Anticipation</u> 1-4, <u>Communication</u> 4-2, and <u>Visualization</u> 2-8.

- Jason begins to set up a new system for Judy (4). As he does, he <u>communicates</u> what is learned back to the point when new needs are being defined (2). He incorporates what the real estate company needs, too.

- Jason <u>visualizes</u> the perfect system at point 8 in order to decide what is ideal for Judy.

- Jason tries to <u>actualize</u> the highest quality modifications (5) to create a system that will be usable and presentable.

- He <u>presents</u> the new system to Judy and her business in a productive way that encourages immediate acceptance and use by Judy, her assistant, and others who need it.

- Judy is left to begin <u>restoring</u> her office to incorporate the new system and its equipment, as well as to remove the old system— after necessary file transfers and backups.

A system upgrade is best accomplished with the Six Secrets and the nine steps working in unison. The timeline is the circle. If the time it takes Jason to upgrade to the new system is too extensive, the whole process will fail. If it takes too long, Judy may as well wait until the next batch of new technology, but by then, business might be lost due to inefficiency.

Jason is the expert at upgrades and will continuously circulate through the process along the lines of the Compass while Judy experiences the timeline at its own pace. Jason's circulation can occur thousands of times while the upgrade occurs only once. Comparing these relative times gives us the impression that the expert moves quickly through a process that appears to move slowly. Time is relative.

Most processes have holes or cracks where the details fail to connect with the real needs of the activity. Yes, it may sound funny, but activities have needs. People adapt and courteously pretend that completion has been attained because they do not see the needs of the activity. They can't quite put their finger on it, yet they feel the incompleteness. Most people do not rock the boat, and yet wish for change. If all who wish for change would rock their boats, we would have bouncy waters.

Controlling the Six Secrets to achieve a harmonious upgrade is essential for any business. But how many systems upgrade professionals succeed? How often are we able to understand their communications?

Ready, Set, Go!

It is not possible to create one set of rules that will sequence every activity using the form of the NTS. In fact, to attempt to do so would be contrary to the meaning derived from the symbol. Every process is unique and each requires some flexibility with the definitions presented in this system. This flexibility is one of the lessons offered from the system. It is one of the "Ah-Ha's."

Flexibility corresponds to reality. To give your expertise one final definition would be to rob it of all creativity. The NTS gives you the ability to interpret your events simultaneously from different points of view. This way of seeing, which includes both thinking and feeling, deepens one's knowledge and intensifies one's striving to understand. It depicts both diversity and unity within a process.

Yet, there are some oversimplifications that may be useful in developing the flexibility to see processes using the form of the NTS. Although the following is an oversimplified way of looking at the NTS, it shows one way of homing in on some processes. It will be useful for us to consider as long as we remember that there are also many other ways of looking at the Nine Term Symbol.

Those who succeed are naturally concerned with the Six Secrets that run in the background, behind the scenes. What the NTS will do for you is to bring these background, magic-making connections to your conscious attention so that you can adeptly steer the wheel of process transformation to success.

Ready Set Go

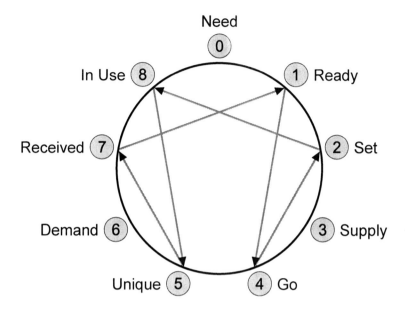

Figure 32 - Ready, Set, Go (without Compass labels)

Look at the Context Triangle: *Need, Supply* and *Demand*. These forces act on any activity involving a product for sale. This clarifies the present scenario; it tells us we are connecting with a process involving a human need. People in companies selling power (electricity, gas, fuel), managing money (banks, mortgages, portfolios) and producing food (groceries, farms, dairy) understand the endless need for their products, which may be a matter of life or death. They *feel* supply and demand.

Does the scenario of producing a unique product for sale follow the "Ready Set Go" model? Let's see:

- The point of being ready (1) refers to the office, the factory, the land, or the field. It is usually a place where people can produce a product.

- The point of getting set (2) refers to setting up the conditions that will yield a harvest or a plentiful crop. The conditions at point 2 must be adjusted based upon what is happening at point 4.

- At point 4, there is full-force-ahead activity leading toward a specific aim. If the tools and materials needed for this full-force-activity were not <u>anticipated</u> (1-4) early on, it would be tough to cross the great divide between point 4 (go)—when everything is active—to point 5 (becomes unique).

- At point 5, the understanding of how the product is in use (8) affects the quality brought into the production that makes this product unique (5). This is <u>actualization</u>.

<u>Visualization</u> (2-8) leads to <u>actualization</u> (8-5) with greater quality. Once you get ready, set everything up and begin to engage in the activity-that-will-make-something (4), you also have to know what the aim is (8) and work to <u>actualize</u> it (8-5) at point 5 (becomes unique). When a product becomes unique, it is because you understand how people will use it at point 8 and how to bring this understanding into the final forging of creation at point 5.

Once you have a unique product, you must <u>present</u> it (5-7) or all will come to a screeching halt. <u>Presentation</u> applies to documentation, marketing, packaging, and sales. You have to take it past the point of being unique and into the place of being sought after.

As soon as the product is sent forth and received by customers, the <u>restoration</u> (7-1) begins. This act of <u>Restoration</u> includes the words re-orientation, re-evaluation and more. (See our ever expanding list of words on page 58.)

And finally, the product is in use (8). But for it to be in use, someone had to <u>visualize</u> this "use" and fully understand the product's usefulness. Online software companies that label their works as BETA are admitting that the "use" at point 8 changes as they observe how we use their products. The legal verbiage (that they ask us to agree with in order to get to the next screen and use their products) protects them as they watch us. They learn about point 8 while we use their products at points 7 and 8. While this is happening, they are continuing to produce—adding to the process at points 2, 4, and 5. They make changes and additions while the product is in use. Once it is improved, they add it to the mix and see how we respond to the new <u>presentation</u> (5-7).

Now, look at the same sequence with the addition of the labeled Compass and picture the Six Secrets at work.

Ready Set Go

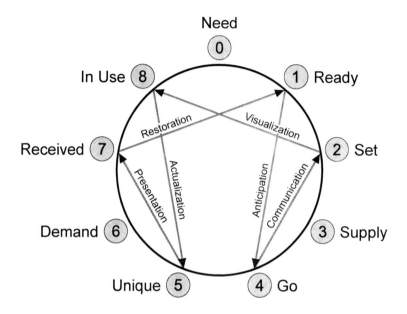

Figure 33 - Ready, Set, Go NTS

At this juncture, if you have followed everything leading up to this, you can read the "Ready Set Go" process simply by reading the symbol. If you imagine an event or a product coming into being on the "Ready Set Go" NTS, you can see the patterns of the NTS at work. Simply picture an activity that corresponds and outline the process using this model. As you compare this symbol to the ones before it, you will find connections with some, but not all, of the processes we have discussed. This is because the NTS is used to express infinite varieties of transformations within the many contexts of business, art, science, and life.

CHAPTER 9

New Way of Thinking

Seeing the Whole

On the first day of Art 101 during my freshman year of high school, our teacher began his class by showing us how to open our drawing tablet to the first page and clip it onto our easel. Once we all had our blank slates in front of us, he walked into the middle of the classroom, looked right at me, and in front of the whole class, he said, "Steffan, I am going to teach you how to SEE."

This shocked me, and I have never forgotten the moment. I thought I *could* see. I had eyes. I could see the white paper. I tried to imagine what he meant, and I drew a blank. I could not fathom it. This teacher was Robert Fulghum, and he had a connection to art and to seeing that I wanted for myself. Over the next four years, I enrolled in every class he offered. There were many of us "Fulghum fans" who followed his stories and advice to our academic and personal benefit. This was years before he became a world-famous author, which came as no surprise to us, since his way of teaching art through "seeing" was pure magic.

By the time I discovered the Nine Term Symbol, Robert Fulghum was my advisor, and I was enrolled in his advanced art history class during my senior year. Studying art with Mr. Fulghum included the study of math, geometry, and symbolism in ancient art, among many other subjects. I cannot say I had learned how to see, but his classes helped me recognize the magic in the geometry and meaning of the Nine Term Symbol. There was something mysterious about the symbol that connected back to what he told me on my first day of art class that freshman year. There was something about "seeing."

Now I can tell you that the Nine Term Symbol provides a pattern that keeps your mind continually fresh, completely out of the box, and yet in close relationship with your process. If we keep thinking in the same way we've always thought in the past, we'll always get the same results. Thinking in new ways causes new ideas, realizations, and abilities to spontaneously emerge.

But the NTS challenges more than just thought; it gives you a way of seeing the whole while connecting with the parts. This stretches your capacity to see, which is invigorating. Seeing the whole while maintaining attention on the parts requires the intelligences of thinking, feeling, and sensing. It feels good to stretch your mind and use your different intelligences. You can't just think your way through the NTS—you've got to feel and sense it, too.

When it comes to business, we need more balance. We tend to overemphasize our Left Brain, the rational thinking part of the mind. Working with the Nine Term Symbol establishes greater balance between our capacities; it engages the Right Brain, too. Our different intelligences are invoked, and the Six Secrets of the Inner Compass show us how, when, and where to apply our intelligences. The more proficient we become at applying the NTS to real life situations, the more quickly we will use it to see any *whole* and bring intelligence into its parts.

> The symbol gives you a shortcut for holding three major factors together: the Circle, the Triangle, and the Compass. These three ideas occur in different time spans. Experts move at lightning speed through the lines of the Compass many times while moving at a methodical pace around the timeline of the Circle. As we have seen, the Circle represents the chronological sequence, the Triangle represents three different supporting inputs, and the Compass stands for the Six Secrets. Each of these patterns in consort helps you move your process toward completion with excellence.

By learning to simultaneously include what is *meant* by each of the factors into your present moment, you see the whole along with its parts in a new way. This new seeing helps you cooperate with the structure rather than fight against it. It helps you take action.

Special Significance

We know something of what is meant by these three geometric patterns now—and yet, there is a special significance contained within the geometry. In ancient times, the mathematics contained within the NTS represented the idea that each point of a process contains the essence of all of the other points, along with the formula for the whole. In modern times, we have holograms, fractals, and string theory to explain the interconnectedness of things. If you have not come across these subjects yet, let me briefly explain them.

A hologram gives us a three dimensional picture of an object. It is a recording of the interference pattern made from two laser beams colliding under specific conditions in relation to the object. One beam bounces off the object and collides with the second laser beam. The pattern they make is stored on a film. When the film is illuminated by a laser beam, or, in some cases by a bright light, you see a three dimensional image of the original object that looks real. It appears to be in the space in front of you, but when you try to touch it, your hand moves right through the object. It seems like magic.

There is another remarkable aspect of holograms. If you divide a holographic film into two halves, you see the entire image of the object from either half of the film. When you divide those halves into more pieces, you still see the entire object through any one of the smaller pieces of film. Because each part of the film contains all of the information that makes up the whole, when you illuminate a small piece of the holographic film, you see the same object in its entirety just as you would if you were to look at the original uncut film.

Fractals demonstrate a similar principal and reveal another magical way to view the world. Fractal math demonstrates that a simple formula can create an infinitely complex pattern. This pattern, when magnified to any level, will show a likeness of the original formula in its parts, again and again, forever and ever. As the pattern generated by the fractal formula grows in size, you can focus in on a small area of the pattern, magnify it to fill your screen, and see that it looks nearly identical to the original pattern.

Superstring theory—string theory for short—is a framework of modern physics that strives to provide an explanation for everything and suggests that all material is a reflection of the same master equation. String theory posits that every atom is made up of particles that are made up of strings. A string is a vibrating loop and can look like a wave, or when it forms a circle, it can look like a particle. What makes strings differ is their pattern of vibrations. Strings vibrate either at different frequencies or at complimentary frequencies, and combine in patterns that produce phenomena. (Any observable occurrence or experience is a phenomenon.)

Before this theory, it was supposed that each different fundamental particle was a "different material." Now string theorists imagine that every particle and every force may prove to be reduced to strings with different resonant patterns of vibration.

These scientific examples illustrate the idea that in each of the parts you can find the pattern for the whole. And as you divide the whole into smaller and smaller parts, you continue to find the whole even in the smallest part. Although the ideas represented by the NTS have been understood since ancient times, within modern science this notion of wholeness appears to be new. The science backing this notion is responsible for new inventions and greater efficiency in our material world today.

Now, with the NTS, business has a tool that encompasses the same notions and can harness these ideas for process transformation. This is important because these ideas are the framework for successful evolution, efficient progress, sustainable transformation, and, quite simply, "things that work." You want these ideas to be your framework as well. **When you look at your process using the Nine Term Symbol, you are working with a pattern that demonstrates these very same properties of physics: infinite variety and compact efficiency.**

At this point, we will dig into the math. It's fun, but if math is not your favorite subject, you may decide to skip ahead and jump in at the next section, "Powerful Pattern."

Wondrous Math

The mathematics of the Nine Term Symbol shares insights with modern science. Ancient thinkers understood the principle of finding the whole within the part by using the NTS. The most striking example is the math of the Compass. It comes from the equation of one divided by seven, which equals .142857142857..., repeating forever.

At the same time, the Triangle of the symbol shows one as divided into three. One represents the whole; the entire circle; a cycle.

Triangle Math

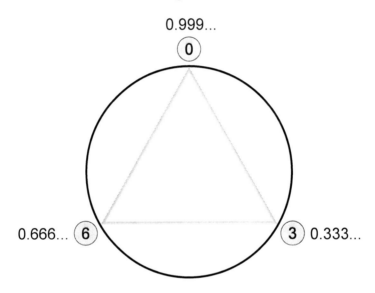

Figure 34 - Triangle Math

One divided by three can be seen as 1/3, 2/3 and 3/3 or .33333..., .66666..., and .99999.... (.99999... is equal to 1.) Each third represents a part of the Context Triangle—the three forces that are independent from, and yet contribute to, the whole.

Important activities are "ones," "wholes," or "cycles." If evolving, they recur with added improvements and perfections with every intelligent repetition. The structure connecting all of the parts of our important business and personal activities can be seen by looking at ONE as THREE (the Triangle) while simultaneously experiencing ONE as divided by SEVEN (the Compass).

Ancient visionaries realized that any given phenomenon could be divided into three, and that all cycles could also be divided into seven points of concentration before reaching the next beginning point. Seeing a whole event as coming from three forces, and also as divided by seven became a key to understanding the harmonious development of a creative act or an evolving process.

The study of octaves and the diatonic scale (string vibrations in music) was used to demonstrate these mathematical relationships and to transmit ancient teachings containing these insights. An evolving process was seen to follow the pattern of an octave in that an octave begins at one note, goes through six steps, and arrives on the seventh step at exactly double the frequency. When you have one note that is vibrating at 440 and another at 880, you have the same note. This idea is symbolized by the apex of the Triangle in the NTS. The beginning is the same as the end, but they are two different places like the notes A440 and A880 are the same, only one octave apart.

The law of octaves (like the law of three) is another great idea presented by Gurdjieff. His original ideas about this are described in the book that, as I have already mentioned, inspired me in my formative years. The very title of that book, *In Search of the Miraculous*, would interest anyone seeking to accomplish the seemingly impossible. A more complete understanding of octaves is useful when you have multiple Nine Term Symbols that overlap one another. In fact, an important concept concerning the octaves of the NTS is that each point of the Triangle is the beginning of a process that has its very own NTS. But looking at the NTS as overlapping octaves is not required to get started and to really make use of its power. We must, as it is said, draw a line somewhere, so, in the interests of simplicity, I will only mention this study here.

We can think of the NTS as an emblem that represents actual laws. Our magical mind has the ability to see a pattern and then form a resonant image of a law that describes the pattern. This ability is itself extraordinary. Using this kind of extraordinary intelligence to form images of universal laws is, in my opinion, how the NTS was created. On an ordinary level, we now use it to improve our activities. But can we also use it to look at the structure of these laws?

When we divide a whole by seven, we get six repeating and circulating numbers that go on forever. To ancient thinkers who understood the significance of this math and connected it with the idea of three inputs contributing to everything, it symbolized the simultaneous being and becoming of all that exists.

Each point of the Compass, therefore, represents one more seventh of the whole in succession. Notice the same sequence of numbers in each of these equations: 1/7th = .142857..., 2/7th = .285714..., 3/7th = .428571..., 4/7th = .571428..., 5/7th = .714285..., 6/7th = .857142... (all repeating forever). When we add 1/7th to 6/7th to make ONE, we get .999999..., which is the apex of the Triangle.

A whole divided into sevenths gives you six sevenths before arriving back at 1. And at each of the six sevenths, we find the same six digits in the same order; the only difference being that they begin at a different starting point of the infinitely repeating sequence.

The inner lines of the Compass follow this pattern; the arrows on the lines depict the direction derived from connecting the numbers in their sequence. If we picture the six increments on the NTS we see the following pattern. The decimal is omitted for simplicity.

Compass Math

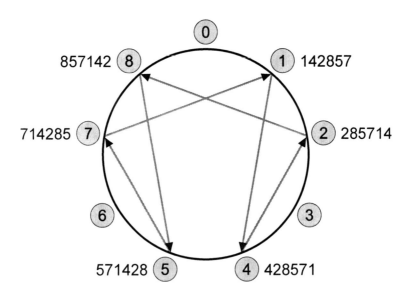

Figure 35 - Compass Math

It goes deeper. To picture the ingenuity hidden in the depth of this math, put your finger on Point One and then move it along the inner lines to each proceeding point (following the directional arrows) all the way back to One. While you did that, you came to each number in the sequence: 1-4-2-8-5-7-1.

There are only six digits in this sequence and only six spots in the pattern of the repeating sequence. As you touched each point on the circle, at one level deeper, right underneath the tip of your finger, the six digits that make up the numbers of each point were "shifting places."

Each individual digit was at one time located at each and every one of the six spots in the sequence. They were taking each other's place until each digit had been in the exact place of each of the other digits in the sequence. Since there are only six digits and only six points, they did their "shifting" in the most efficient way possible—in only six steps.

The magical idea is that at each of these six points, we find the same pattern of numbers repeating forever. Each begins with a different number: the number that corresponds to that specific point on the symbol. (Point 1 begins 142857, point 2 begins 285714, point 4 begins 428571, etc...) Each of the six digits fills the place of each of the other digits in the sequence. All this happens in six even increments, six simple steps. And when you look at the whole symbol, the circle with the inner lines connecting the points 1-4-2-8-5-7, you are looking at the very same formula seen within each of the points. The whole demonstrates the pattern of the points and each point shows the formula for the whole.

Powerful Pattern

The math contains a clear metaphor. As we stand at each point of our process, we are connected with all of the other points from within the very point at which we are standing. Each point contains all of the same parts. Each point contains all of the others, and in each of the others there exists another complete replica of all of the others, and so on to infinite magnitudes. The master formula for the whole is found at each individual point.

The idea that each point of the process contains a similitude of the whole and a likeness to every other point should not be surprising to an expert. Experts know that at every point of their process there is a real sense of what is happening at every other point. This sense is not because the process is predictable.

Instead, there is an amazing amount of imperfection in an expertise. There is room for growth; there is uncertainty and spontaneity as well. The only predictable fact is that the expert can guide the process toward perfection as it moves to completion. This is because the expert has repeated the process enough to find ways to perfect it. The expert will adjust for growth and spontaneity and will navigate to success. Whether he knows it or not, he has found the master formula.

The expert uses the Six Secrets to guide the whole process while he works diligently at each point. When he is aware of this and can use the Nine Term Symbol to aid his connectedness and his seeing, he has a powerful, efficient tool guiding his progress.

It should be clear that we have been talking only about these six points and not about points 0, 3, and 6, which are the points of the Triangle. The point labeled "0" can also be seen as "9" since it clearly represents both the beginning and the end. These digits are never found in the recurring pattern of 1-4-2-8-5-7.

We have been viewing this math without dividing the space around the circle into even sevenths. We have been leaving room for the three digits of the Triangle on the Circle while looking at just one of the ideas by itself: the math of the Compass. The Nine Term Symbol connects several patterns into one.

The powerful pattern contains the idea that our impulses to accomplish our aims will deflect (the Compass) along the way to completion, (the Circle) and that there are distinct points where we need to allow for inputs from outside (the Triangle). Independent or self sufficient events follow this pattern. And because this pattern includes inputs, we might rather say that nothing evolves or is self organizing unless it is in harmony with this pattern.

The NTS combines the idea that every whole event requires three inputs with the idea that every whole naturally develops along six points of concentration between its beginning and its end. This combination of Laws makes magic for those who know the secret: the resulting form and sequence.

NTS Math

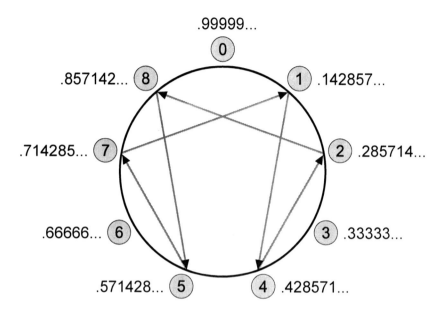

Figure 36 - NTS Math

Indeed, there is more to this symbol than the math of the inner lines of the Compass. The Circle has meaning as it draws a line between what is and what is not included in a process.

The Triangle also has meaning. It represents three necessary inputs with the contrasting qualities of affirmation, receptivity, and equilibration. Experts find all three of these factors, whereas most people see one or, at most, two. The Triangle illustrates the fact that opposite values are complimentary. We will explore this in more detail later on, but right now, we turn to another discovery of science that validates the benefits of working with the NTS both personally and in business: the hemispheres of the brain.

Left and Right Brain Thinking

Our brains have two hemispheres, one on the left and one on the right. Scientists have proven the two hemispheres exist, and that each is responsible for completely different types of activities. Each approaches our processes with entirely different skill sets. The Left Brain functions with logic and analysis, while the Right Brain functions with imagery and synthesis.

The hemispheres are connected. We never do anything without both sides of our brain. We do not act solely from our Left Brain when we analyze statistics, nor do we compose music solely from the Right Brain. Instead, our actions come from a blending of both brains. We can say that the Left or Right Brain controls an activity, and that the other side of the brain influences that same activity.

Most businesses have favored Left Brain logic, and there is a strong bias toward valuing Left Brain thinking in our information age society. However, those who can use their talents for synthesis, seeing the big picture, creating artistic designs, and empathizing with others (all Right Brain activities) are in increasing demand. People want products that move them emotionally as well as perform a purpose.

The Left Brain is still more active, more valued, and more accepted in our society. Yet, in order to have an effective business, in order to make the right choices in life, one has to use and integrate both sides of the brain. The Nine Term Symbol depicts the integration of both sides of the brain simultaneously. It values both equally.

The Nine Term Symbol with its "1-4-2-8-5-7" shows us a picture of our Left and Right Brains at work within a process. The numbers are logical, sequential and mathematical (Left Brain thinking). Our Left Brain is required for the circle: at each of the points Left Brain qualities are required to get the tasks done. And the inner line pattern of the Compass moving through the process uses qualities from the Right Brain: creativeness, synthesis, and simultaneous connectedness. The circle is sequential: directed by Left Brain activity, and the inner lines are qualitative: directed by Right Brain activity.

Right Brain thinking is useful for synthesizing, caring, and connecting disparate parts of a whole together, thus bringing insight, quality, and empathy to a process. The lines of the Compass represent these types of activities. Even though they are lines, they do indeed represent the non-linear approach to process integration. Our ability to synthesize rather than analyze, our ability to see the patterns that connect our activities rather than the list of sequential events, and our aptitudes for seeing the whole, finding meaning, and caring for creation are all qualities inherent in the inner recurring pattern of the Compass.

The Nine Term Symbol not only provides us with a way to describe our expertise, to understand a process, and to share our understanding with others, but it also acts as a tool for helping us develop our Right Brain. In general, we are underdeveloped in our Right Brain thinking and overdeveloped in our Left Brain thinking. The Nine Term Symbol asks us to use both hemispheres of our brain together. If we are in the minority who are not overdeveloped in our Left Brain thinking, then we probably need validation for our Right Brain thinking in this left-brained-world. We may also benefit from seeing the practical usefulness of the Right Brain, which the NTS can provide. The NTS shows that Right Brain thinking connects with linear, Left Brain patterns. It also shows *how* and *where* Right Brain thinking connects with Left Brain patterns.

In the upcoming section describing what Role or Type is useful at each Position (see Chapter 13), we will recognize that the NTS also provides a way for Left Brain thinkers and Right Brain thinkers to effectively communicate. It helps various types of thinkers to understand and value each other more fully. The NTS will help us build greater respect for one another when we identify the Roles we must play to move our work forward.

Keeping It Simple

What this all boils down to is that we can improve our business or personal processes using this symbol. The NTS offers a unique, succinct, precise form to help us master the accelerating changes and transformations in our process-oriented world. These are the processes that will determine whether we succeed or fail in our endeavors, and these are the processes that need our attention. Experts improve their work with this pattern, and if we are not an expert, we can use the NTS to become one. By using the NTS as our framework, it is easy to transfer abilities and mastery from a familiar experience to any new field or a new process.

In summary, we can proceed with the idea that by using this symbol to understand our processes, benefits will accumulate through challenges to our mind and our intelligences. With the combination of patterns in the NTS, we are following the laws that make processes work and evolve. One of the reasons this helps us refine our activities is that at each point there is a wholeness not found in other ordinary techniques. We are more deeply connected with our process when we use the NTS, and the Six Secrets, to clarify the whole. These built-in factors will naturally support our efforts as we forge ahead and apply this symbol to create process transformation.

Strengthen the Secrets to Improve the Whole

Having considered these somewhat lofty concepts, let's get back to basics. We will now look at several important business processes and apply the Six Secrets to their development. And we will begin with a new approach: the idea that if we only improve our ability to work with the Six Secrets, *this is enough*. We do not need to be conscious of all of the math, the science, or the hemispheres of our brains. We just need to improve our work by being guided by the Symbol and the Six Secrets. Simply put, when we strengthen the Secrets to improve the whole, the rest will follow.

With this in mind, as we proceed, our minds will now look at the NTS with an unlabeled Compass and instinctively think like this:

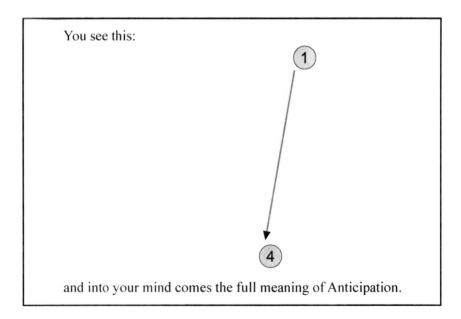

You see this:

and into your mind comes the full meaning of Anticipation.

You see this:

and your mind connects with Communication.

You see this:

and you sense the notion of Visualization.

And this:

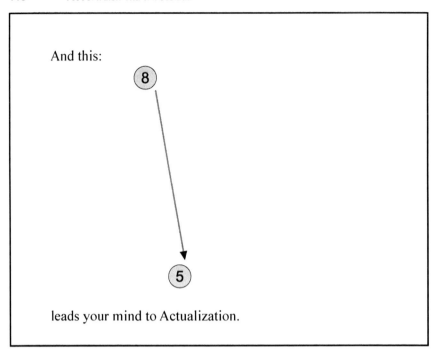

leads your mind to Actualization.

This:

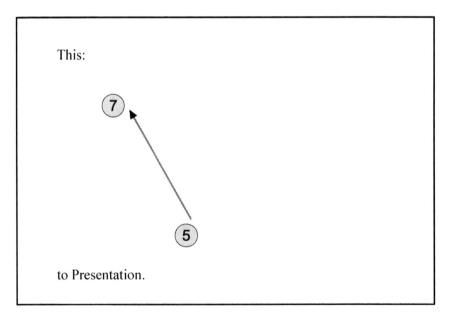

to Presentation.

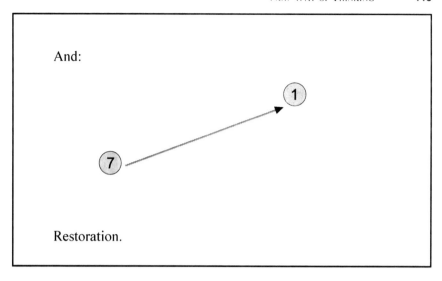

Once you have memorized the Six Secrets—which happens naturally as you follow along with this book—it will become intuitive to read the NTS with or without the labels on the Inner Compass. This will lead you to new territory.

ᴄꙅ◊ꙅꙩ

Watching someone present an NTS of a process can be revealing and—like magic—a bit amazing. When you watch a magic effect, you are only amazed if you do not know how it is accomplished. When the NTS is shown, you must know how it works to be amazed.

Magic tricks are nothing but procedures, ingenious procedures that allow the spontaneous experience of wonder for the spectators. What it takes to perform these ingenious procedures is awe inspiring. But those who investigate the methods involved soon lose their sense of wonder.

Think about this for a moment. The effort it takes to perform a magic trick can itself be amazing due in part to the ingenuity involved in the procedures and in part to the skills that are needed to pull it off. But that is not what is amazing at a magic show. Learning the secrets causes people to lose their sense of amazement when they see the effect performed. They soon become disenchanted, unless they begin to see how clever the process actually is.

Instead of being amazed by the trick, the learned spectator may become amazed by the skill of the magician and the ingenuity of the process designed to inspire awe in the minds and hearts of the laymen. But, this kind of appreciation does not happen if the spectator learns the secret while the performance is going on. That occurs either when a mistake is made by the magician or when the spectator just plain figures it out. A good magician keeps both from occurring and that is what is so challenging about the art. What it takes to keep everything on track is ingenious.

There is great depth involved no matter which way we look at magic trick procedures. And this has provided endless fascination for me since I study the effects of magic from all sides: the methods and procedures, the minds of the spectators, and the nature and consequences of the experience of astonishment!

So, what is so incredible about it? In every magic trick, there are two paths that are taken, one by the performer and the other by the spectator. The magician weaves a circuitous route while the spectator follows an apparent step by step road to amazement. By the end, the two paths meet in astonishment. The magician's aim comes true and the spectator enters into wonder.

If a spectator is not willing to be surprised or if he comes to the event with strong doubts, the results will vary. Even one person with a negative attitude can affect the show. But a good magician can entertain even the toughest, most skeptical group.

Does any of this sound familiar? A magic effect is like the Nine Term Symbol. The NTS has a "circuitous" route in the Compass, a step by step route in the Circle Timeline, and it allows for everyone's unique inputs with its Context Triangle. The magician has to think ahead at every turn. The spectator has to follow along. And the three inputs of the Triangle: the magician's skill, the spectator's mind and the experience of wonder must all come together in one whole.

My concern for the art and my interest in the nature of process are compatible. The reciprocal relationship with these two passions is that each provides experiences for the other to grow. They feed on one another. We will return to this later on.

We have now described enough about how the Nine Term Symbol works for there to be another reward. The stage is set for us to be amazed that we can actually see a multitude of processes using just this one form. With our initial efforts behind us, we are prepared to uncover many different types of processes using the NTS.

CHAPTER 10

NTS Models in Brief

Corporate Training is big business. Six Sigma draws a crowd when large companies want to measure improvement. Health is in high demand as the baby boomers age, environmental toxins increase, and nutrients in our food supply decline. Independent laboratories running tests for doctors and hospitals are thriving. Computer programmers are designing more useful and intuitive software than ever before. Corporate events and trade shows have become more refined. Communications specialists face challenges—with the new media, electronic communications, and public image—and are demanding greater efficiency and sensitivity. Increasing regulations impose burdens on organizations that ingenuity must overcome. Each of these concepts and many more can be outlined and interpreted with the Circle Timeline, the Context Triangle, and the Compass of the NTS.

Because you have the language of the NTS, you can now create outlines for a wide range of activities that offer a wealth of information to anyone who knows the language. You can look at symbols made by your collaborators and instantly see their point of view. If you are a leader with insights, you can now convey them in a conceptual form that will allow for public challenges, feedback and improvements. Sharing understanding using the NTS as a common language with collaborators will highlight areas of agreement, misunderstanding, concern and efficiency. You may see areas that work as well as those needing improvement or polishing. All of these benefits are major indicators of a learning organization.

Why do we want this? In groups of collaborators, in business and in life, intentions conflict; different interpretations come from the same facts; errors in management, shortsightedness and disputes are commonplace. For most of us, our state of mind is more often in fixed opinions than in openness. Our points of view must remain open and fluid if they are to respond with creativity to the demands of the present moment. The NTS helps us organize our mind which increases our openness and the potential for innovation. The state of mind that leads to solutions pushes the barriers of the impossible. Our magical mind leads to immeasurable results.

Each NTS below compresses numerous aspects of its process within the framework. By considering the Circle Timeline, the Context Triangle and the Compass, you can choose which ones to unpack and explore in greater depth. The NTS is shorthand for those who can read its code.

Training

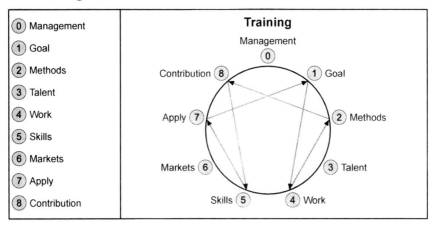

Figure 37 - Training - list & NTS

Working in the corporate event business exposes one to the aims of management and the ideologies that achieve their goals. What the training department has to accomplish is outlined by the Compass while the typical procedure is outlined by the Circle Timeline. The Context Triangle shows the drama. Training experts must take their direction from management (0) and work with their human resources (talent–3) to prepare them for specific business needs (markets–6).

Every training session has a goal: what the student will learn or accomplish. The trainers draw from methods that will help students develop skills. These skills will lead the student to the ultimate aim of making contributions on their own in the business environment.

When the student's skills meet real events in the marketplace, the training is applied and a contribution is achieved. Here management can succeed along with the trainer. But the trainer must move swiftly amidst the lines of the Compass to keep this activity constantly in check.

The corporate trainer must:

- Know the Goal

- Anticipate the session: the Work

- Understand the Methods

- Know how to adapt the Methods for the Contribution

- Know when to adapt the Methods for the Talent

- Communicate in order to adapt the Methods and the Work

- Visualize the Contribution

- Actualize the learning of new Skills

- Teach how to Present the Skills to Markets

- Reevaluate the Goal along the line of Restoration as the Skills are Applied

Training

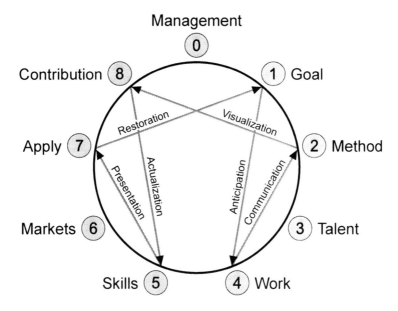

Figure 38 - Training NTS

Take this to your next training session to see if you can find ways to describe your actual experience.

Six Sigma

The NTS reveals complexities involved with large organizations.

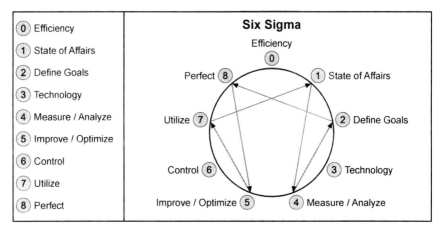

Figure 39 - Six Sigma - list & NTS

The team implementing a Six Sigma plan within an organization follows the lines of the Compass along with the procedures involved on the Circle Timeline. The technology comes from many sources. Scientific controls placed on the system aim to produce fewer errors. As the system is optimized, it is presented through controls to the point where it can be utilized and then gradually perfected.

We use the word "perfect" with a specific meaning. Continuous improvement practices can help us perfect a process. Here we do not refer to unobtainable perfection. We do mean that although something is not perfect, we can be involved in perfecting it. A thing can be perfected to a degree that is not yet perfect.

("Six Sigma" is a registered trademark of Motorola, Inc. The phrase has become common, and in this example, we refer to general ideas pertaining to the common use of the phrase.)

Six Sigma

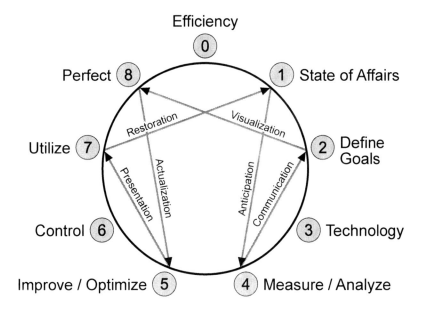

Figure 40 - Six Sigma NTS

Healing

Doctors are not only scientists; there is an art to healing.

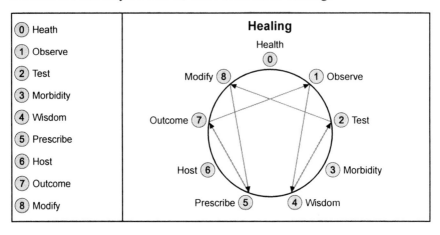

Figure 41 - Healing - list & NTS

Health is the equilibrium between morbidity, which is the rate of incidence of disease, and the host which is the body. Every disease requires a body (the host), and health is restored through processes. The Context Triangle is omnipresent. The factors of the Triangle do not enter the timeline as much as they are always there. This is easy to imagine when it comes to healing in that the body, the disease, and the state of health are there at every step of the way.

A doctor looks into the wisdom (4) gathered from the profession to decide what tests are important. She can picture what modifications are likely, and will prescribe a treatment plan to cure the patient. But the outcome (7) must be examined before the healing process reaches the point of skillful modification (8). The choices arising from this point of modification must come from a blending of factors from both patient and doctor.

Healing

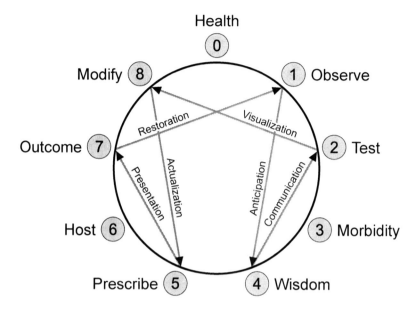

Figure 42 - Healing NTS

Laboratory

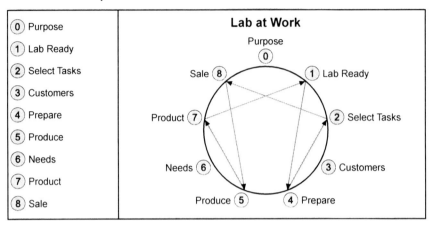

Figure 43 - Laboratory - list & NTS

Have you ever read your blood test results? To most of us, they are printed in a foreign language.

What happens in the lab must not stay in the lab. The lab manager works along the lines of the Inner Compass to control the quality of the tests and the flow of business while the activities of the staff aim to accomplish the points of the Timeline.

From all over the lab's vicinity, doctors and patients send in samples every day. Their needs range from critical to casual. The purpose of the lab is an immediate and accessible mission statement including real people making a living and serving their community. The employees as well as the lab's wide variety of customers all meet at point 0.

While the production phase (5) moves toward point 7 to become a product, the needs of all parties must be served and "presented to". If you have tried to read your blood test results and then compared what you see to what your doctor shows you from the same report, you will appreciate the need for presentation (5-7). Test results that everyone can understand are of greater value and in higher demand than results in codes that only experts can interpret.

Finally, the products are sold and sent out to doctors to aid with their diagnostics and prescriptions. The lab recovers, replenishes and restores as early as (but not limited to) point 7 and continues this line (7-1) until it is ready to begin again at point 1.

Lab at Work

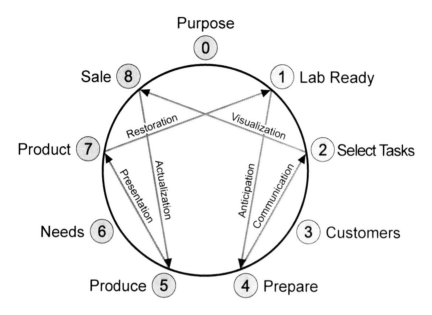

Figure 44 - Lab at Work NTS

Product Development

Creating software follows this basic pattern.

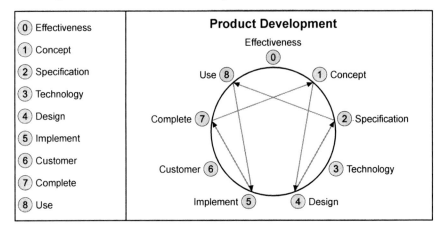

Figure 45 - Product Development - list & NTS

The overarching need for effectiveness helps integrate technology with the customer. Point 8 refers to the new product in use. This "use" must be visualized early on and continuously funneled into the making of the code segments at point 5. The codes must work together without bugs, and the customer must test the product before it can be completed.

There are many variations of this model. Each development team must make adjustments to this symbol to reflect the scope and scale of their work. If you are an expert in this field, and you look at this NTS and then begin to make changes to it, you are involving yourself in exactly what this system encourages.

Product Development

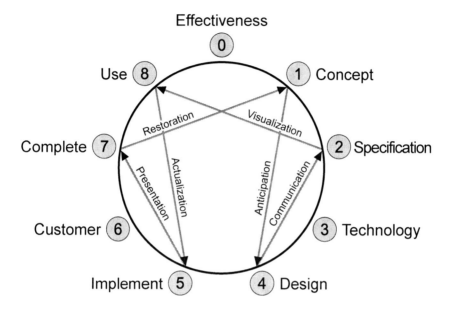

Figure 46 - Product Development NTS

Event Production

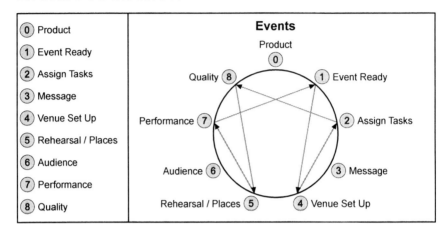

Figure 47 - Events - list & NTS

This is a corporate event at which messages reach an audience for the purpose of promoting and selling products. Point 0 refers to the totality of products, tangible and intangible, that pertain to the event. The event producers adjust to the venue, monitor the quality of the event and actualize that quality at point 5 before the audience arrives. The speakers and performers must take their places (5) and present their parts to the audience. Once the session has taken place, the audience, speakers, performers, and the event planners realize the quality of the event.

This example begins with the event fully planned. We can apply this pattern to a convention, symposium, seminar, conference or trade show. The event may repeat and travel to multiple venues. The entire conference takes place between points 5 and 7, but requires major efforts before and after this critical portion of the Circle Timeline.

In the 1990's, a major hotel chain hired me to perform for the board of Meeting Planners International for the purpose of impressing them with an outstanding show. At that time, event planners were gaining recognition. They were needed, but they had to prove their value. I started in the corporate event business just prior to this trend, and I have learned to distinguish between fads and lasting improvements. My feeling now is that event planning has been repeated and studied to the point where high quality events are predictable and comfortable. This industry will always need to bring new blood, fresh approaches and magic into events and meetings. If you plan events, you can use the NTS in your event planning sessions to guide the indefinable process of pulling creativity out of thin air.

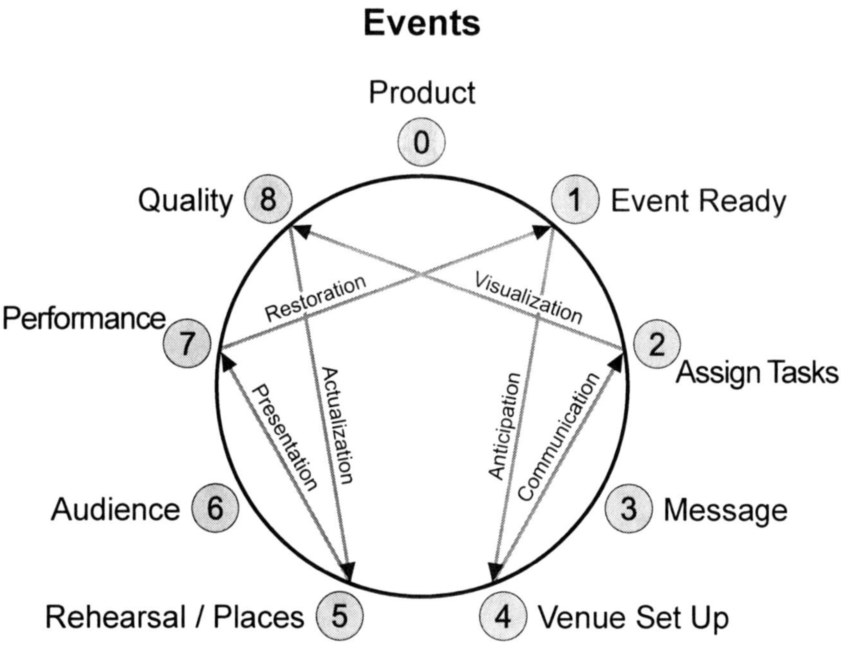

Events

Figure 48 - Events NTS

Communications

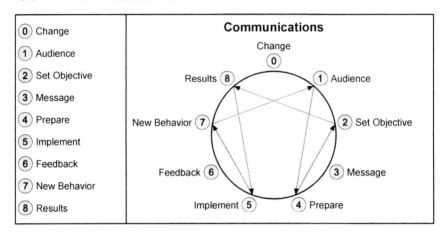

Figure 49 - Communications - list & NTS

The communications expert will <u>anticipate</u> the type of campaign that needs to be prepared in tandem with understanding the impending change, the audience, the message and the objective. Much relies on <u>anticipation</u> in this particular process, but experts fail unless they can <u>visualize</u> a measurable result that can be <u>actualized</u> in the practical world.

While the message is being put into a campaign at point 4, <u>communication</u> about the media (what forms the campaign will take), the timing and the objectives must be continuous. At the same time, measurable results must be planned for (<u>visualized</u>). This requires deep insight into how the audience will respond (6) as they provide feedback and make a judgment that leads to a new behavior. The expert wants to know how the audience is changing while the campaign is being <u>presented</u>. This measurement can be arrived at (<u>actualized</u>) only if the campaign is implemented with built in benchmarks for results. Just counting the number of hits a website gets does not measure real results. The expert will dig deeper.

As the audience demonstrates a new behavior, the reevaluation and <u>restoration</u> phase gets underway. If not, the circle must begin again and possibly compensate for errors during the next round.

Communications

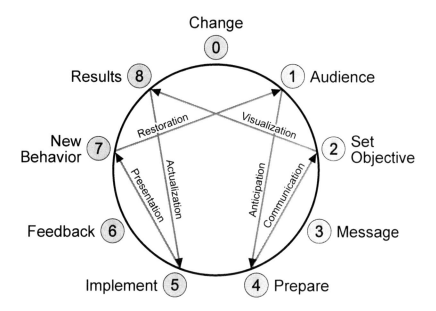

Figure 50 - Communications NTS

Network Marketing

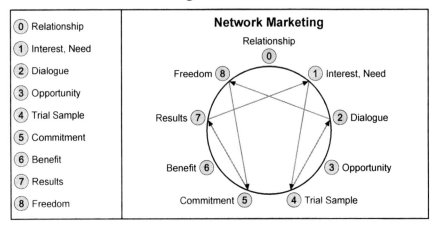

Figure 51 - Network Marketing - list & NTS

Network Marketing or Direct Selling is also called Multi-Level Marketing (MLM). It is an important business model to understand. It is studied in business schools and produces billions in sales every year.

The entire business starts and ends with relationships. The sales person studies how to look for interest or a need in those with whom they come in contact or have a relationship. They open a dialogue about the product stressing the opportunity, give the potential customer a free sample and hope that the customer will commit to a trial period. During this time, the customer will experience the benefits of the product which will produce positive results and lead to some added freedom. This could be freedom in the sense of improved health or even financial freedom if the business takes off.

Successful products sold in this way are usually superior to comparable products obtained through traditional channels. The company offering products through a direct selling system does not have to spend as much on marketing and can therefore create a higher quality product for a price that is competitive. When customers experience the higher quality products, they realize that it is a better deal and continue ordering with their representative or directly from the company itself.

Network Marketing

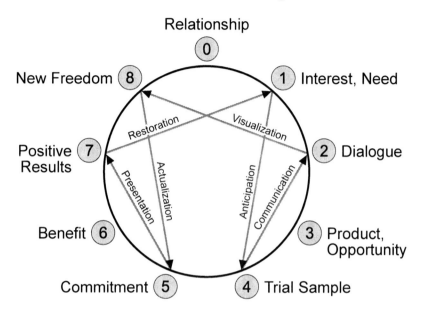

Figure 52 - Network Marketing NTS

While the Six Secrets are fairly self explanatory in this NTS, I will say that the line of Communication refers to the reactions that the potential customer has to the product and the opportunity. This reaction tells the sales person specifically what to speak about and how to direct the dialogue.

And the line of Actualization may need some explanation. The new freedom is real. High quality nutrition for example can make a big impact on people especially given the state of nutrition within our modern food supply. The fact that many people can make a little extra money and those who take it seriously can make a good income is also a possible freedom. It is this potential that actualizes the commitment to give the product and/or the opportunity a serious try.

Conflict Resolution

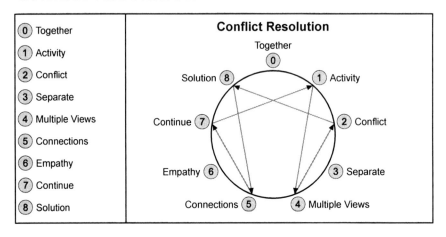

Figure 53 - Conflict Resolution - list & NTS

One of the greatest benefits of using the NTS is you only have to translate a few words to share an idea. In other words, you do not have to accompany lengthy descriptions with every NTS. The symbol describes the idea if it is well labeled. Sometimes all you need to describe is your meaning of the words you have chosen to act as labels. The user can then read the process from your perspective without much of a description.

In this example, a careful study of the Inner Compass shows how we can use conflict for personal gain. By entering into the conflict through communication (4-2), picturing solutions (2-8) and trying out new connections (8-5), we set up the conditions for developing new perspectives within ourselves at point 6.

Conflict Building

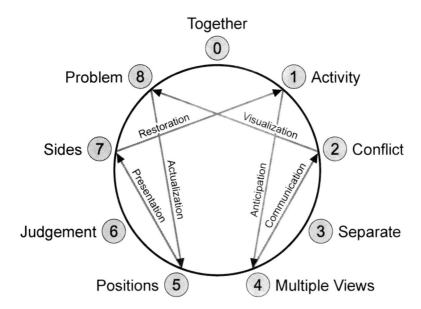

Figure 54 - Conflict Building NTS

To understand conflict resolution, it helps to see how conflicts continue. Notice the similarity between the two symbols—conflict building and conflict resolution. The right side is the same for each, but the **left sides differ**. The left side can be used to create positions, make judgments and take sides which will likely emphasize the problem, or it can be used to make new connections and continue towards a solution. Groups may have to repeat points 1 through 5 numerous times before they find the way to continue (7).

The conflict I am referring to in this scenario is one belonging to a process that everyone involved would like to continue. If this were about a process that was not appropriate, that would be a different story. The idea of "together" at point 0/9 is simple and not some idealistic form of togetherness. The fact that people work together enters into this equation and will be an active force in keeping the process alive.

Conflict Resolution

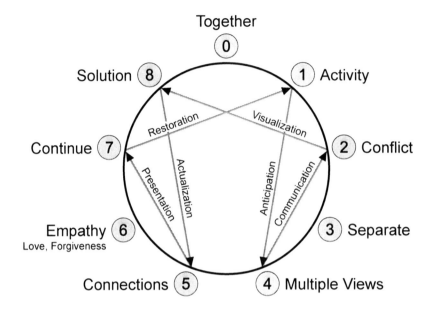

Figure 55 - Conflict Resolution NTS

The ideas of love and forgiveness may seem like an impossible dream or words that do not belong in a business board room, but no, they are in fact a reality. Even a brief investigation into how empathy, love and forgiveness forge business relationships that change the world will demonstrate to anyone in doubt that these words belong. It is true however that we must practice this point of the process before we can claim that we have love or forgiveness in our situation. In the fields of religion, psychology, spirituality, and even law, there are many sources for learning how to attain this state of being, and the NTS serves as an outline for applying those methods.

Fixing the Education System

In the United States math and science scores of high school students are at an all time low, and over one million high schoolers drop out every year. Our society and our economy will benefit from better preparing our young people for success. There are strong needs to find new structures that work in order to transform our failing education system.

As I read Scott Oki's book on transforming public education entitled *Outrageous Learning*, I came up with several Nine Term Symbols. When I revisited these symbols a year later to prepare for a performance I was giving to a major educational institution, I was able to quickly reconnect with the ideas from his book that I had found valuable.

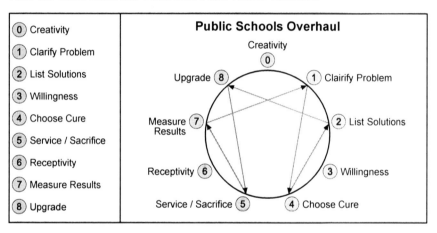

Figure 56 - Public Schools Overhaul - list & NTS

Public School Overhaul

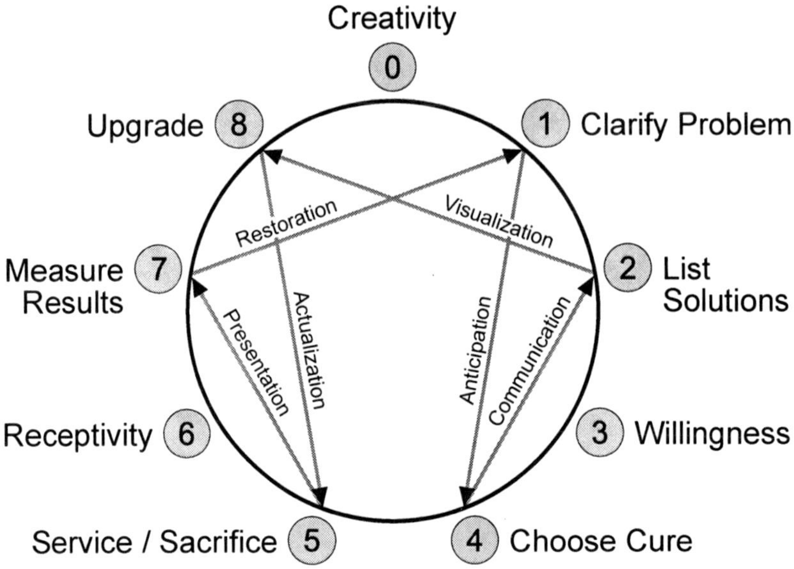

Figure 57 - Public Schools Overhaul NTS

For an honest upgrade to occur and not just another set of regulations, Creativity must enter the scenario. For this, there must be a Willingness that is active and a Receptivity to change. With this Context Triangle of forces it would be possible for an overhaul team to meet and move around the Circle Timeline to point 5 where the system will either make it or break it.

Real service and honest sacrifices will undoubtedly play a large role in the future of our education system. As Oki says, we need to enlist a large group of volunteers and get to work assisting our teachers in the classrooms in a variety of ways.

Public School Transformation

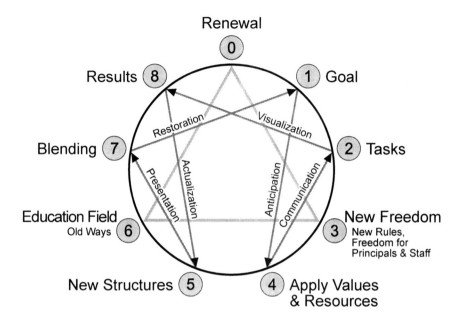

Figure 58 - Public Schools Transformation NTS

Here we can see how the forces of the Triangle again play the essential role. Sometimes change can be brought about just by lining up the three forces, standing back, and letting the timeline run itself. In this case that would mean giving everyone involved three kinds of willingness: for renewal (0), to allow new structures to replace old ones (6) and to take the responsibility that comes with the freedom to make improvements at a local level (3).

The Compass adds real depth here as we define one who is "task oriented" (someone working at point 2) as one who keeps tasks broadly focused on Results and narrowly focused on application (Applying Values and Resources). We see that for Results to happen, we must respect the old system as a force to reckon with (6). The Education Field must accept the reforms that can blend with it for sustainable Results. The Goals will differ from the practical Results. Tasks at point two will come from Goals but aim for Results. Our Goals will be redefined by the process initiated at point 6 that includes the Compass action points of 5, 7 and 8.

The large scale transformation needed to raise the level of our public schools is a gigantic undertaking and may require the kind of large scale thinking accessible with the NTS.

Insanely Great Teacher

One of the key ideas in Oki's education manifesto is that we need "insanely great teachers". His focus is on creating the right external influences to attract these types of teachers. Since he does not say what actually makes a teacher great, I offer my impressions as one who's been influenced by many incredible teachers. In the following NTS I am also influenced by John Bennett's "Realization of Beauty" chapter from his book *Enneagram Studies*.

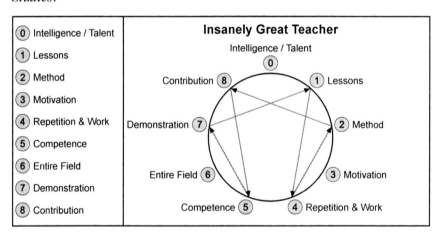

Figure 59 - Insanely Great Teacher - list & NTS

The Teacher moves from point 1 to point 4 to monitor and adjust the Method (2). While studying (points 1, 2 and 4), the student may experience some insight and a Motivation to learn (3) can appear. Great teachers aim to inspire a student's wish to learn. They want a student to feel a sense of self satisfaction within the act learning.

Once the Repetition and Work (4) bring a student to being "pretty good," the possibility of the student's future Contribution (8) to the field brings hope during the long haul from good to great. This is when the outside world of other experts and the vast body of knowledge within the particular field of study will show the student where refinements and improvements are needed. This process of the student's competency "meeting the field" in Demonstrations (7) through the line of Presentation will lead toward independence from the original teacher. It is at point 7 that teachers move on to the next class of students.

If a student develops further and makes the necessary sacrifices to enter into the deeper levels of her field, she may make a Contribution to the field at large. The act of Contribution (8) is a reward for a great teacher and will motivate them to remain in the trenches of the classroom. While this motivation for the teacher is an important ingredient, it is long term. The short term reward, which is the sign of a great teacher, is the light that ignites in the student who finds a sense of "I can" or who experiences the feeling of "learning is fun." Great teachers continuously look for and create little switches that will turn on this light.

Insanely Great Teacher

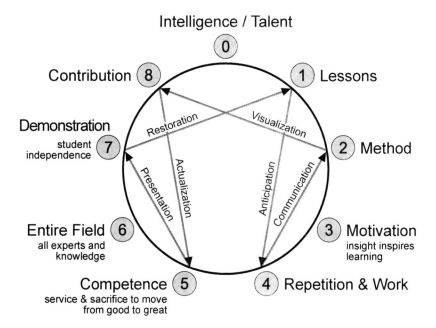

Figure 60 - Insanely Great Teacher NTS

Real Estate - CMA

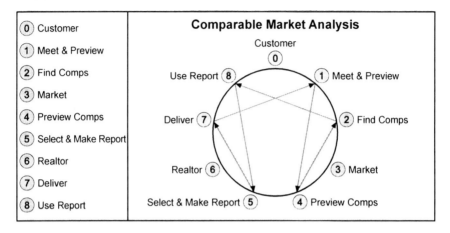

Figure 61 - Real Estate CMA - list & NTS

The realtor moves along the timeline with attention on the inner lines of the Compass. As soon as she meets her customer and the customer's house, she is <u>looking ahead</u> to what she must find in a comparable ("a comp"). Several comps are needed to determine the market rate for the customer's property. She knows the area, the neighborhoods, the rhythm of the market. In her awareness are factors that contribute to intuitive choices unmatched by computer algorithms.

While viewing a comp, she must <u>take notes and adjust her search</u> at point 2. The actual use of the report varies based upon some clients wanting to know their net worth and others wanting to sell. The entire process will be simplified if it is <u>aimed</u> at what the report will be used for, the true purpose.

Once the best comps for the client's aims are actualized, the realtor selects the data for the report, and begins to put it into a presentable form. The research includes recently sold properties as well as current houses on the market. The <u>presentation</u> may need to be high quality, or it may need to be done with no frills. This <u>actualizing</u> of the quality of the report comes from a blending of understanding how the client will use it and what kind of presentation will lead to future business for the realtor.

Point 6 refers to the realtor's tools, her skill and the support she gets from her company. She delivers the report (7), explains it to her client and affirms she can market it for him. She <u>puts her work in files</u>, moves to the next project and hopes to gain a customer when the time is right.

Comparable Market Analysis

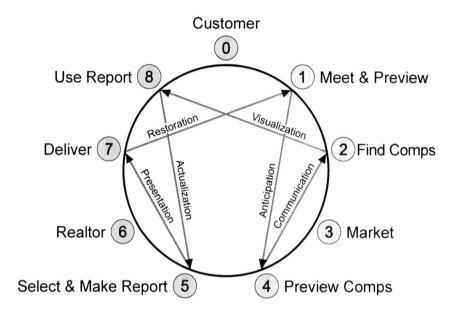

Figure 62 - Real Estate CMA NTS

These Business Briefs could each be an entire chapter, but with the power of the NTS, each entirety can be transmitted to those who wish to pursue it while still remaining concise and providing insight.

Magic Effect Performance

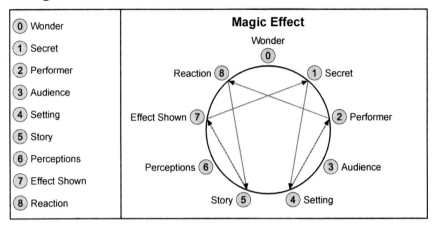

Figure 63 - Magic Effect - list & NTS

The magician begins with a secret. He must <u>understand</u> everything from the angles of the venue to the attitude of the audience, to the lighting in the room. These are factors of point 4, the setting. Careful <u>communication</u> about these factors helps the performer select his material. He <u>aims</u> for the best achievable reaction at point 8. Every effect is selected at point 2 for its impact at point 8 and its feasibility at point 4. This is best done before the audience arrives, but can occur at any time during the show.

The picture of the ultimate reaction helps the magician <u>actualize</u> the most convincing appearance and natural story when the performance begins at point 5. The <u>presentation</u> is aimed at affecting the feelings and perceptions within the minds of the viewers. Everyone has a slightly different experience which leads to subtle adjustments as he gauges the impact his effects have on the audience.

As soon as any effect is shown, the hiding of the secret and the <u>restoring</u> of the expensive materials used to create the effect begins. It is here that the audience digests the experience and arrives at an overall reaction. The magician wants them to remember the show for the rest of their lives, and can attain this aim only through intense dedication to the process and continuous improvement. All six of the Secrets must be balanced for a great performance to take place.

Magic Effect

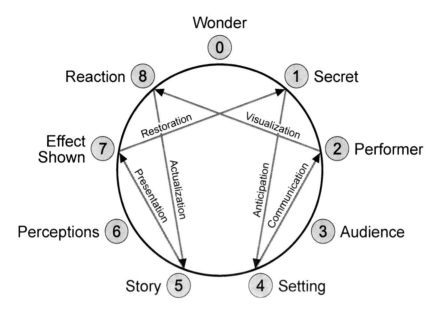

Figure 64 - Magic Effect NTS

The fastest way to master the power of the NTS is to learn to think like a magician.

CHAPTER 11

Overlapping Processes

Think NTS

When processes overlap, you might think it will be challenging to create a workable NTS. But processes overlap, and though you may not have realized it, the NTS has been showing us this idea from the start. Each of the three points of the Context Triangle represents an independent process. Each of these three independent processes is supporting the one process we are viewing on the NTS. We also know that there is activity at each point of the Compass. These activities may also be processes that can have their own NTS. It is not difficult to see that processes overlap. There will be many Nine Term Symbols used to express a variety of functions in an organization where people communicate to accomplish projects.

In these times of great scientific knowledge and understanding, the complexity of interactions between multiple processes—that make up any whole—requires constant attention if we are to establish patterns and structures that function for all their intended purposes.

An organization may be complicated, but you do not need a completed NTS before you can use its lessons to improve your projects. In my business we create productions in machine shops and rehearsal halls that are then advertised and marketed to buyers and subsequently presented in front of audiences in theatres and multimedia. Merely thinking along the lines of the NTS helps our interactions whether or not we have a symbol in front of us. In fact, it would slow us down to keep pulling out our NTS to discuss what's happening.

It is more important for individuals to apply the qualities represented by the Six Secrets to their work than to analyze their NTS. The NTS proves, for instance, that it is reasonable to spend time looking into the future to ponder a better way to Actualize a higher quality product. Just knowing that it is okay to Visualize for a few minutes is of great value. Putting more energy into Anticipation can clear up Communication errors that were wasting time before. Without this model, these time expenditures might have been completely ignored or dismissed as frivolous.

The NTS is a tool that efficiently guides you along the pattern that experts use whether they know it or not. You do not need a completed NTS in front of you to realize when an important Communication is taking place. Chances are this communication is on the line of 4-2 in someone's process. You do not need the NTS to see that your brochure must be redesigned because it does not serve the audience or the message. Chances are you are near point 5 and working on Presentation.

In these moments, you can improve with the understanding that your work is bound to be in line with the Inner Compass. It is bound simply because it is a process. You can proceed knowing that if you strengthen any one of the Six Secrets, in any one project, even if you have not mapped it out, you will strengthen the whole project.

This phenomenon is referred to as "NTS Thinking" because the mind is thinking with the principles of the NTS. This works effectively within overlapping processes. When you view an activity on the NTS, you do so in order to gain and share understanding, but do not stop there. Within any important activity, you can apply values from the Six Secrets and maintain a sense of what effort is needed to manage the whole process. You do not need a symbol for every occasion. The lessons from NTS Thinking apply to many moments and endless situations.

Overlapping Magic

These days when I pull a rabbit out of my hat it refers to performing an outstanding number of complex effects for a sophisticated audience in impossible circumstances. It is not easy, and yet, I manage to do it all the time. I am talking about simultaneous layers of complications:

- a laptop with 100 sound & light cues triggered by a wireless button sewn into my costume to create a musical beginning, middle and end for each piece

- roller shades drawn over the bottom of a cage where doves wait in the dark to be released the instant my assistant presses the lever

- stage hands listening to my stage manager call the cues in the headset to raise, lower, stack or extend any one of five curtains

If a stage hand does not understand or is unrehearsed, the curtain not raised can keep the audience waiting for what seems like minutes. Or, on the other hand, a curtain raised before its time can reveal a trap door being set.

It is show business, and it's challenging to manage. If my arm presses too tightly against a secret button, I can accidentally trigger the wrong music, and nothing will be as rehearsed for the next five minutes unless we reset the laptop which is way up in the control booth. To reset, I would have to walk through the audience of 1000 people who bought tickets to see me and ask them to bear with us while I fix the music. It happened once, and once is enough to put a refinement in place, to study the system, to augment the process.

The doves do not just get uncovered when the roller shade releases. There is a net at the end of a four foot pole. I am swooping it through the air when a dove appears inside the net. It looks that way, but it's more complex. It involves a dove which I make disappear at precisely the moment that the one appears fluttering her wings inside the cage.

My assistant's thumb on the lever controls the live dove release mechanism. If the split second timing is blown, so is the magic, because the audience will see two doves at once. An ice skater can get up from a fall and continue with grace, but when anything happens that reveals the secret, a magician can seldom regain the confidence of his audience.

When I am about to address a packed theatre of people who have driven from all over the vicinity, bought tickets to "Steffan Soule's Dreams, Magic & Miracles," and expect to be entertained for 90 minutes, I am not standing calmly in the wings waiting to be introduced. Instead I am hiding in the dark while my dance team spins me in circles. While spinning, I move up through layers of secret materials into an awkward sitting position. My face is now inches from a 200 watt bulb in front of which I present my hands to make shadows on a screen that is about to be removed as I magically appear.

You can hear the sound of astonishment before the sound of applause as the audience embraces the first magical moment of the show. I am now sitting in a pyramid that was just empty. The dancers grab my hands and counterbalance my weight. I stand and step down to the floor which is the signal for the final music to play. This ending music is triggered by me squeezing the secret button to activate the wireless signal that tells the show software to go to the next series of cross-fades and light cues. Sound glamorous? I need my hands free. It's show-business, and when we can do the sound & light cues in house it saves labor costs.

There are eight counts from that transition to the blackout. During these eight counts, the dancers spin into place around me while I strike a pose guaranteed to bring another round of applause for the same effect. But only if each of the preceding cues were executed at exactly the right times, in the proper form and sequence … . Is it any wonder that I became involved in understanding process and interested in continuous improvement?

Since all of my magic effects are hand-crafted, rehearsed, marketed as part of a show, and then finally presented in front of a live audience, it should be possible to see connections between these overlapping processes using the NTS.

The builder builds the effect. The manager markets the show. The performer provides the experience.

A magician works with builders and managers. The magician performs with the materials he acquires from the builders, at events arranged by the managers. Some magicians try to build and manage, and some magicians focus mainly on performing. I am an inventor and not a builder. I collaborate with builders to achieve original works, so I know their process. I am a manager, having successfully operated my own company since high school, and I am a performer. To look at how my business functions, I made these three symbols centered around the builder, the manager and the performer.

Within the Context Triangle of the building of magic, the *reliability* part has to do with being practical, sturdy, transportable and usable. The *method* has to do with the ways to accomplish magic. These secret methods are known, documented and continually studied. The *materials* make the effect possible when they're put together in a certain order.

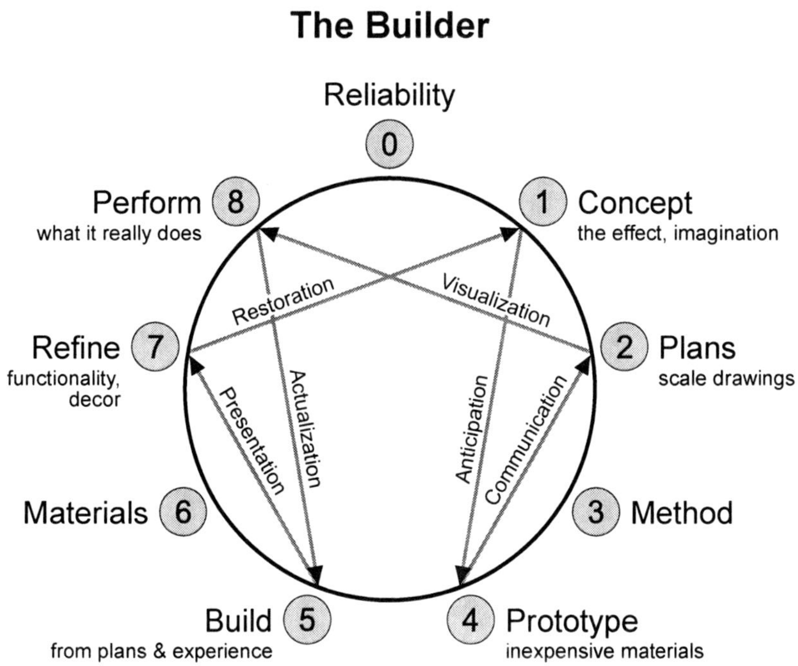

The Builder

Figure 65 - The Builder, Building Presentations

The builder starts with the concept then anticipates how he's going to make the prototype. The prototype informs the plans that will become scale drawings. As he's drawing up the plans, he has to imagine the performer performing the effect. This helps him actualize the building process. It helps him to enhance the possibility of the performer having a perfect product. There are many things that can go wrong during a performance, and the builder can prevent many failures. At the point when he's building, the materials come into play. At point 7 he is refining the product, finishing it and putting the surfaces together so it looks attractive to the audience. The inside of a prop may not be seen by the audience and may remain unfinished, but the mechanisms on the inside require special skills to build and to refine.

The Manager

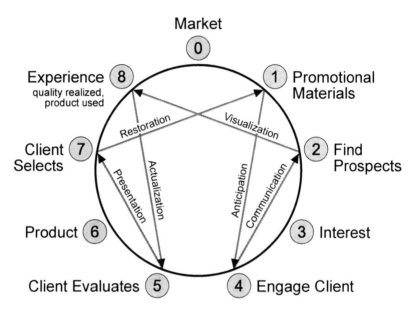

Figure 66 - The Manager, Marketing Productions

The manager has to start with good promotional materials. He looks ahead to engagements he thinks he can get and to clients he thinks he can interest. He communicates this back to point 2 where he finds prospects. As he's finding prospects, he's visualizing the total experience at point 8 where the client and the product are unified. With this positive image he can actualize the evaluation phase with that client and help steer it. The product with all of its production value comes into play. It has to be a high quality production for it to succeed. Then at point 7, the client selects the performer, and at point 8, the client and the performer have their experience.

The Performer

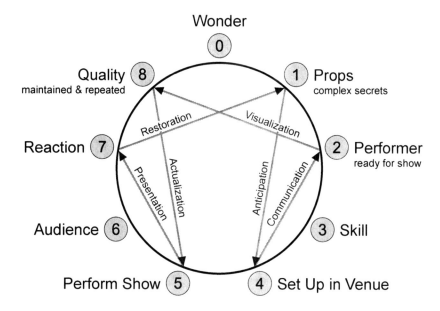

Figure 67 - The Performer. Performing Presentations

The performer goes through his process beginning with his props that cost tens of thousands of dollars for every three to five minutes of show time. He ends his activity by restoring them back into custom road cases to head to the next venue. Every audience will have a different experience, and he is only as good as his last presentation. A performer can't call in sick and can never miss a show. The quality must be maintained throughout the experience and repeated endlessly.

The performer is mainly creative, whereas the builder is mainly practical, and the manager is mainly efficient. So we have practical, creative and efficient persons all working on the same team.

Each of these overlap. To see this, you will need to look at all three symbols and consider the connections. Point 1 of the build (concept) must be planned by a vision of points 6, 7, 8 & 0 of the performer. In other words, the performer must know what reaction he can get from an audience and understand how to achieve astonishment (wonder), and this must be embedded in the concept at point 1 of the build. The success of the build goes into point 1 of the performance. When a magician has a reliable prop, his job is easier. Point 8 of the building NTS (perform) is where the quality is realized in the process. It is here that the prop transfers from the builder's hands into the hands of the magician. And the quality of the prop can affect more than just one point of the performing NTS, but it enters into the performing NTS as early as point 1.

The quality of the prop may also enter into the promotional materials which is point 1 of the marketing NTS. Point 6 of the marketing NTS (product) is certainly based on the quality of the performer's production (point 8 of the performing NTS).

The builder's quality affects the show's quality. Point 8 for the builder (perform) affects point 1 of the performer (props). The builder's quality, at point 8, affects the show's quality. And the performer's point 8 affects the manager's point 1 because promotional materials are based on the quality of the performance. The quality of the show affects the promotional materials.

Art and Business

Magic has shaped my mind. The art, the business and the NTS have penetrated my thoughts and influenced the way I perceive things. They have given me reasons to bring my different intelligences together: to feel, move and think in consort.

To create the effect of a miracle or impossibility demands a special effort. It is similar to learning how to be a pianist or an actor, but requires the added dimension of props: specially made secret items that must be precisely manipulated without anyone becoming the wiser.

Of all the effects I have produced during my life as a professional magician, the most miraculous would have to be making a living at it. A good living at that. And by the way, one does not need fame to be full time in the arts. There are hundreds of great performers who work hard and make a good living while remaining in the background at events. In fact, fame leads to expectations, whereas not being famous helps a performer blend in and deliver a surprise. For me, making a living performing magic is especially good because I do what I love. Even after ups and downs in life, I remain passionate about the art.

Running the business is a different story. While the results of business are exciting, it is not always easy to be passionate about the daily tasks. Fortunately, there is some art to any business. Probably due to the fact that I see the art in my business, I have always enjoyed the detail and the repetition that goes along with serving the needs of my business—from cleaning the dove cage to writing the computer code that generates a report from the database.

My business and my art both rely on recurring processes and my ability to maintain the parts that link the whole. The demands of running my own business, in which I play the lead role, as well as the manager, can be overwhelming. There have been years when I have performed shows non-stop while neglecting paperwork. And there have been years when there were more papers moving across my desk than there were clients booking events. At every period it has required attention to detail and a mind for process integration.

To succeed in business, especially in the arts, you have to be efficient. You have to anticipate the solutions ahead of time, see where processes overlap, find new ways to communicate and always be willing to bring things back to a restoration point from which the process can begin anew.

The same is true for presenting a magic show. When you are a magician, your skill at moving through the process is almost more valuable than your ability to perform the trick. There are hundreds of secrets. The magician has to insert his secrets into the process and use them at the right time or the audience will not be amazed.

The audience moves through the presentation in chronological time and the magician moves through the process with three times: before, during and after. His secrets are set up before the audience enters. The tricks are performed during the strictly controlled presentation, and afterward, there must be a lingering sense of wonder. If you do not leave the show astonished or impressed by the apparent impossibility, then there is no magic.

The NTS reveals that the real secret of the magic show lies in the magician's ability to move through the process in a completely different way than the audience. This applies equally to any expertise, any business. And it all boils down to how we work with process, something with which I've always been fascinated.

Seeing Gaps

As a young magician, I was naturally attracted to the discovery of anything that might help with the actualization of intended results. I was always on the lookout for ways to accomplish the seemingly impossible. I was keen to find a secret that might help me or anyone manifest a vision or make a dream come true. I knew how hard it was to make even one moment seem like magic, so I was bound to have respect for a technique that would truly work if I found one. I was also highly critical of methods that used suggestive language to create impressions of effectiveness because I could see through most any illusion. The truth is that the NTS seemed magical to me when I found it, but it took many years of working with it before I realized its powerful significance.

My understanding of magic and the NTS has led me to see processes in a different way than most. My primary aim during a performance is to induce wonder. I am convinced that neuroscience will discover the role of wonder in the brain. It seems like a chemical reaction occurs in the audience during a show when wonder appears. As a professional dedicated to improving my performance, I have developed a sensitivity to the conditions that create wonder. These conditions include timing, the flow of events, open-mindedness, closed-mindedness, people's psychology, people's relationship to the impossible, architecture, lighting, sound and more. As a student of the NTS, I notice that many human endeavors are filled with a series of incomplete processes that we interpret as complete when the results appear to be as intended. Many processes stop just before or right after one of the points of the Triangle. Some are simply missing any real depth of qualities from the Inner Compass.

Consequently, I have developed the ability to see into the timing of situations and find the gaps—the moments of less attention—into which I can insert a secret from my profession that can help me produce astonishment in my audience. Some people call this "mis-direction"; I call it "directed attention". There are psychological gaps or collective gaps in attentiveness in any period of time with any group of people. The art of magic is a discipline and the presentation of the art requires specifically controlled environments along with directed attention.

Due to my unique combination of interests, I constantly notice process in action. I have spent time mapping various processes on the

NTS in order to "see efficiency" and find "efficiency gaps". Efficiency is magical. It is practical too, because when you have it, stress disappears and everything flows. I suppose many people who run their own business and deal with interrelating processes become efficiency experts to some degree. This requires an open mind that is dedicated to detail, which—if you think about it and try to experience it—appears contradictory, but the NTS reconciles being open minded with being mindful of details.

Crisis Responsiveness

I have not received a call from the CIA or the FBI to solve a crime or create a camouflage system for a secret spy mission yet, but it might happen. Magicians actually serve in these fields. In fact, you would probably be surprised to know, magicians have helped with critical military missions. Some basic principles that magicians spend a long time mastering can be used for everything from understanding crimes to driving secret missions. It seems to me, as I watch the news and read the papers, that we could use the NTS to see where we fall short in everything from managing a crisis to attempts at improving dangerous traffic conditions. It is a logical supposition that the NTS can be used to map out a potential hazard as well as how to manage a crisis.

The NTS of responding to a crisis would need many examples, and each scenario may require vastly different overlapping symbols. In recent famous crises we can see a lack of Communication and Visualization. When the Twin Towers fell in New York, the emergency response teams on the ground could not communicate between agencies. This was combined with an inability to see the big picture (line 2-8 in a crisis) of what areas were in trouble and specifically what kind of trouble. The lack in these lines led to the tragic and unnecessary deaths of emergency responders. Communications are critical in the midst of a crisis. Although the CIA had already visualized planes being used as weapons, the line of Visualization never lead to (actualized) a plan for prevention. Major improvements have been created since this attack to intentionally strengthen these lines of Communication, Visualization and Actualization.

Anticipation is a key to preventing a crisis. Mapping out a way to listen for and process the signals indicating that a crisis may arise is a way to use the NTS. The line of Actualization, in this case, would lead to the act of preventing the crisis beginning at point 5. The team that prevents may also be the team that performs in the heat of an actual disaster. If the team is cohesive, we can view the team's actions as initiating an input from outside and entering into an NTS at point 6. Presentation may sound too easy-going for the actions surrounding the need to disarm a crisis, so we can rephrase this line to "Application/Utilization" for instance (see page 58). The act of preventing or responding will bring a crisis to the point of regaining stability which initiates the line of Restoration.

The overlapping processes involved in these vast fields of preparing for emergencies and responding to crises are prime material for teams empowered with NTS Thinking. To view symbols pertaining to this subject, log into your account at AccomplishTheImpossible.com, or make a new account specifically for this purpose, and use the friend system or the search system to search for the word "crisis" or the phrase "crisis management." By sharing symbols concerning specific fields such as crisis responsiveness, NTS users can develop a world of knowledge that leads to a deeper understanding.

Not Your Ordinary Way of Thinking
With the system of the NTS we see things in a new way. This system is a way of thinking, and not the usual way of thinking. Our ordinary way of thinking is necessary but not sufficient. We need the automatic reactivity of our ordinary mind sometimes, but ordinary thinking leads to fixed attitudes and limited understanding of the meaning of things. This keeps the mind from making connections and seeing potential areas of progress.

NTS Thinking is a natural form of Kaizen because improvements happen quickly and even spontaneously with this mindset. The business practice of Kaizen, originally from Japan, results in "change for the better" and the elimination of waste from a process. It takes a practice to bring these results into an organization.

Ordinary thinking reacts predictably but is not proactive without special training. It does not automatically see waste as something to eliminate, for example. With NTS Thinking, waste can be an efficient input for another, overlapping process. Inefficient waste can come from a lack in one of the Six Secrets or a gap in one of the inputs at the points of the Triangle. With the NTS, we see into a world of interconnecting patterns. This awakens our magical mind to find areas for rapid improvements or "change for the better".

Recently I had the opportunity to speak with a raw material manager working on a new airplane. He explained that they were wasting over 90% of their raw material in order to create a particular bend in an aluminum tube with specified tolerances. Five disciplines overlapped: Design, Quality Control, Manufacturing Engineering, Supply Chain, and Manufacturing. All five checked out and everyone agreed they should be producing quality parts without scrap. The only possible point in their process that looked like it must be to blame was Manufacturing. But that team insisted that they were doing it perfectly.

That left the machine itself. Upon experimentation, it was discovered that although the machine was in perfect order, it required material to be within tighter tolerances than the specifications required. A simple call to the suppliers and a small tooling charge created the change in the tubing raw material that eliminated all failures. In a flash, they went from 90% loss to only 3% loss of raw materials.

In the common language of the NTS, point three had an overlapping process that could be changed to fix the process they were examining. This solution was difficult for the teams to see because everyone proved to Quality Control that they were right, and they were. Even the inputs from outside were within specifications. But a change in the input led their machine to function with greater precision.

Sometimes you may find that one of the Six Secrets or one of the points of the Triangle is lacking or is not working in your structure. If for example your line 8-5 (Actualization) is not functioning to the level you require for a successful process, or if it needs boosting, you can label this line with another word or phrase such as "Creating Solutions". This new label will remind your team that it is here that we need new energy, more attention, and solutions to emerge. With this reminder in place, you can work together to focus your extra efforts toward this one need. As the process repeats, everyone is aware and on the lookout during the build up to and the heading out from this one particular phase or line. This will open a door for an improvement to enter the scene even while processes overlap.

When we apply NTS Thinking to systems that are working together, overlapping processes are improved in consort. This is real continuous improvement as the effects of one group's work affects another's. When each group works toward improvements with a common language and shared vision, a synergy develops that carries the organization to new heights.

CHAPTER 12

Self-Improvement and the NTS

Using the NTS can lead to self-improvement. It naturally finds strengths and weaknesses within a process, a process run by people. We would therefore be remiss if we did not examine the transformation of weakness into strength.

I will begin with my own worst weakness. There was a time when smoking was acceptable. As our social consciousness changed and our health awareness improved, smoking became a weakness. To admit you needed nicotine was like announcing you were a liability; just ask any insurance company. As a child, alone at night and drifting off to sleep, I remember the safe feeling created by the smell of cigarette smoke from downstairs. I knew my parents were home and still awake.

Years later, as a professional in the progressive age of health, I felt I had to hide my love of nicotine until I could eventually quit using it all together. While I used it sparingly and with discipline, I really did not like the "me" who needed it, even if I only smoked once a day. So I stopped.

For two months while I was building my strength to refrain from starting again, I kept the following diagram in front of me. I pictured my new self every day, and it worked! I have been free from nicotine for years. Although I still feel the pull, I have transformed a weakness into a strength that has allowed me to resist one of the most addictive substances in the world.

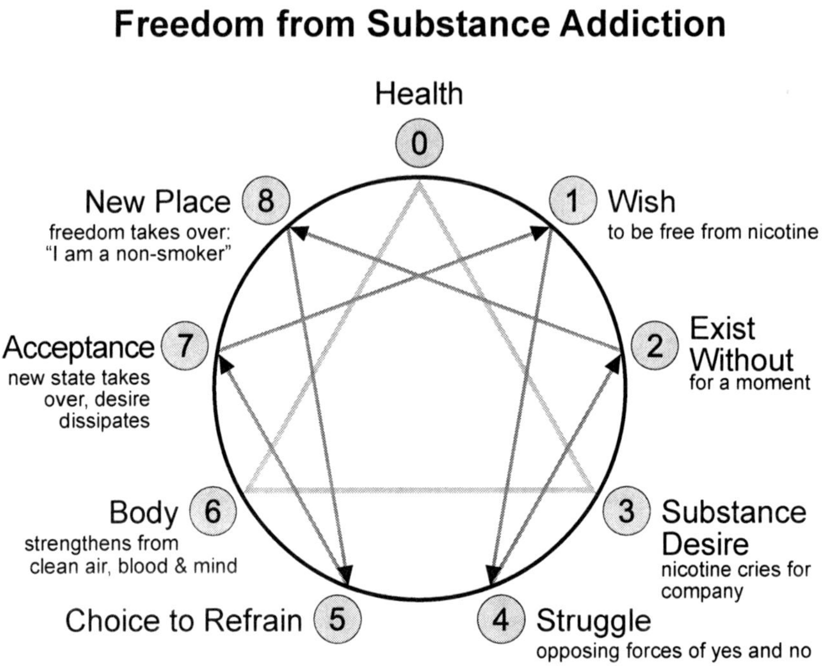

Freedom from Substance Addiction

Figure 68 - Freedom from Substance Abuse NTS

The Nine Term Symbol helped me kick the habit. The principles outlined in this view (Figure 68) connect to the NTS for transforming weakness into strength, which we will discuss later on.

Ego and Egoism—"Check Your Ego at the Door"

To become proficient in my field, I find it necessary to study not only how to improve my external conditions, but also my inner world. Have you ever noticed that real experts seem to keep their ego out of their work—at least for a duration that exceeds others in comparison?

This comes from a wish to create and to give. The wish is to create without any separation of, for example, who is superior and who is inferior, and to give without keeping account of who gave what to the end result. True experts love what they do and want to improve their inner relationship to their work as well as their outer material world.

True experts make their work look effortless. And although their work is certainly not effortless, the appearance of effortlessness is not an illusion. They do not try to make it look effortless to impress us. They have clear intentions, and they smoothly direct their attention to what needs their effort. They allow their process to unfold like a sculptor removing outer layers of rock from the sculpture living inside the stone.

I will always remember the week I spent in Japan watching the world competition of magic. I spent seven days in a dark theatre at the convention center watching non-stop magic performances. There were hundreds from morning to night, and while many were only interesting, just a few were truly good.

I found something to appreciate in every performance, but by the fifth day, I suddenly saw what it was that distinguished the "good" from the "bad." In a word, it was "intentionality." I could see when the intentions of the performer were not executed as he or she had originally intended. There was a subtle recognition, a hint of failure in the performer's postures, gestures, or facial expressions; there was a "tell."

This reaction was also not intended, not part of the ideal performance rehearsed for the judges. This made a double layer of clutter in the sense of unwanted, extraneous actions and signals. The ego knew it was caught. It could be seen because, in the body, there was a reaction to the fact that everything had not gone perfectly as intended. I could clearly see the difference between those who were moving as intended and those whose movements were out of sync with their intentions. I could see they had only rehearsed their external movements and did not rehearse their intentionality. My high school art teacher would have been pleased, for, in his words, I was "seeing."

Performing magic for magicians is nearly impossible. Not only were these brave performers showing their work in front of an audience of magicians from all over the world, but they were in front of experienced judges who would soon state their opinion in the form of a score that would be seen by all. The ability to not be distracted by what the judges will think requires a special state of being—a focus—a freedom from ego.

Nonetheless, some performers did retain a calm presence and appeared to hit their mark. They were "in their body," and they executed each move according to their intention. When I saw this difference, I realized that egoism kills magic. A magician must act from intention, and if a mistake happens, he must not react with tension. He must allow the moment to be. Then he can move into his next posture and manifest his next intended result.

Most audiences do not know what is about to happen or what the magician is intending. If the audience sees something go wrong, they may not recognize it as a mistake. But if they see the magician's ego react to a mistake, they will know he is not connected with wonder, art, or magic. They sense a self concern, the existence of the performer's attitude toward his self or his mistake. This takes the experience to a lower level that cannot produce the chemical reaction of wonder.

The major insight I had into how egoism pollutes the art, and how ego-less-ness propels it, led me to develop a greater freedom with my audiences. I was able to see this in others because I had practiced working with my attention and intention for years prior. Many theatre exercises— given even to beginners—encourage a relaxed attention in the body during postures, gestures, and movements. Of course, another reason I could see this in others is that I was already very familiar with failures and successes during performances; I could taste it. I had seen this wide range of ego qualities from the inside out.

Since this experience in Japan, I intensified my work to increase inner freedom. Using the Nine Term Symbol, I developed a particular method that helps my attention and intention come together. A few years later, I competed and won first place in an international magic competition. Everything went perfectly during the competition, but at the final evening performance, when each of the winners performed in a row, I impressed the audience of magicians with a major mistake. Yes, I say impressed, because when the bottom fell out of my fake candle and exposed the entire insides to everyone, I simply picked up the secret, tossed it inside a hat and kept going. I didn't miss a beat. I did not react. My presence was intact because I was not self-absorbed. Many magicians commented on how I handled that moment like a pro. The audience gasped as if an ice skater had slipped and fallen, but they were right back with me because I got up and started skating again without concern.

Before we examine the specific method that guides the connection of attention and intention to work together, we will recognize a general tendency toward self-improvement already inherent in the NTS: **when we examine our process, we examine ourselves, too**. Because whatever we examine changes in its quality as we examine it, using the NTS naturally leads to improving ourselves. And when we use the NTS, we look at real connections within activities that matter to us. We are, therefore, bound to see our strengths alongside our weaknesses.

When you see your strengths and weaknesses, take note and observe. Do not react like the magicians who did not perform what they intended in rehearsal. That only adds to the clutter. Instead, choose to watch. Resist the idea that you can change a weakness as soon as you see it. Resist the impulse that you must fix a problem or adjust to a weakness right away. This develops your ability to be in a non-comfort-zone. Many actors and performers report that they create their best work when they are not comfortable, when they do not know what is coming next. They find that it is best not to seek comfort by covering for a mistake or adjusting to an error.

Adjustments are effective when they are backed by experience. Experience comes from repetition, and repetition is useless without your attention. If you only repeat your automatic reaction to seeing a weakness, a reaction that strives to adjust, to become comfortable, your experience will remain shallow. When you bear the full experience, you can bring your non-reactive attention into your present moment. This allows you to see your weakness more fully and deepen your understanding of your experience.

If you check your ego at the door before you enter the process, you can get to know yourself from within the experience. Once you know yourself in a whole experience, you can choose another pattern because you know all sides of the experience. You can choose a new way before you get to the old pattern because you are not constantly reacting and adjusting in order to remain in a comfort zone. You are present to your self and your potential improvement ahead of the impulse to adjust.

This brings you to the cutting edge of choice. You make a choice that makes a lasting difference because it comes from your real understanding and not your mental picture that tries to fix things before it sees the whole.

Seeing the whole, including one's weaknesses, requires an extra effort and the confidence to bear the discomfort that will naturally arise. To accomplish this bearing, to endure this discomfort, requires support from your own decision to work this way. You must have enough attention along with the intention to do it.

Understanding grows with a specific kind of follow through. The repeated act of bringing attention into your experience produces the power to notice and observe, which eventually increases your understanding.

The process we are discussing is any one that requires new patterns and self-improvement. When you find factors inhibiting self-improvement, it is useful to focus on your strengths. We need to remember our strong points when we have doubts about our potential for change, have difficulty communicating, or find friction while working in a team. Working with the NTS will equally provide insights into your strengths, both as a team and as connected individuals. These strengths can be observed and called upon when needed to fulfill a task or follow through with an action. They are necessary, but not sufficient. If we only strengthened our strong points, we would be lopsided.

Obviously, the transformation of our weaker patterns into strong points is going to help us, but we also need to study our strengths as part of this process. Our strengths help us see what can be, and knowing our strong points helps us overcome doubts and maintain confidence as we delve into self-transformation.

The Self-Improvement NTS

Let's see if we can picture this on the NTS before we look at the symbol.

We begin with our Self in a state ready to go to work, and we <u>Anticipate</u> our next activity. If we know that there can be weakness during this activity, we <u>Communicate</u> information about this weakness to ourselves in an effort to recognize the potential for change.

At this point, already, our attention is divided. Part of our attention is directed to our activity and part to our inner life. Our attention directed to our inner life becomes the intention to choose.

When we recognize the potential for change, we can <u>Visualize</u> the new pattern that we are aiming for (if we know what that is). If we do not, we send an invisible connection to the new pattern-to-be by merely wishing for it. This picture of the new pattern-to-be helps us to <u>Actualize</u> our understanding and to see what is needed at the present moment when we need to choose. I often speak of this moment as the "present moment" because this is when one's attention is present, and only then can one intend one's actions rather than react.

Armed with our ability to bear the seeing just a little longer than our automatic tendency to adjust, we <u>Present</u> the state of our situation— our current understanding—to the potential choice. We gain insight and see the possibility of creating a lasting difference. We connect with the wisdom leading to lasting change.

The new pattern is now available for us to choose. It will endure when we choose it because it is no longer in the temporary, half-baked form of reactivity. It is ours to use as we see fit. We <u>Renew</u> the Self that began on this journey through our insight and choice of something new. Now we can view the NTS with the Compass labels.

Self-Improvement

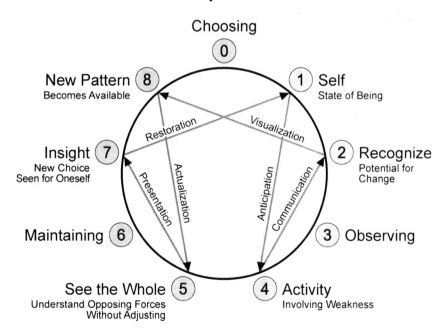

Figure 69 - Self-Improvement NTS

We can also describe the outer form around the timeline: The Self who can improve goes to work. Remembering the potential for change and connecting with the ability to observe precedes the activity where weaknesses may arise. Otherwise, we catch ourselves and try to fix it. No lasting change comes from reacting to the impulse to adjust.

As the weakness arises, we follow it with attention and make an effort to understand the whole picture: to really see the Self in the situation. We maintain this, and over time, insights arise that help us find and choose a new pattern. It is no longer as difficult as it once appeared.

The context of self-improvement revolves around the ability to be passive enough to observe, active enough to maintain (and not adjust or fix), and finally, to choose. These abilities are inherent in the Self, but not activated unless we become aware of the need and bring our attention into the action.

We have to enter the activity with attention and intend something new. We do so through our power of observation, power to maintain our attention in the present moment, and our power of choosing to be involved more deeply than before. Our attention is brought inward and becomes intention. We intend something new. This is how a weakness can be brought into the light of change. It comes from one's own true Self.

In this next symbol, the Triangle is prominent, and we can get a feel for how deeply important it is to see what it points to. In this particular NTS, the Triangle is held together entirely by one's own being. In your being, you have the power to observe and to maintain your attention until you have the freedom to choose. This relates to the wonderful way the NTS depicts the "Development of Learning" as shown in the following chapter.

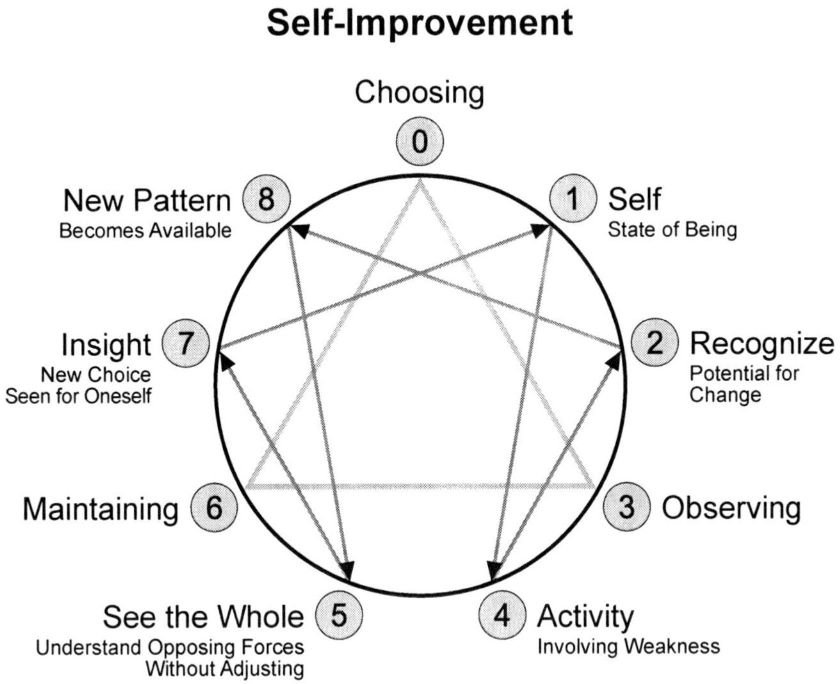

Self-Improvement

Figure 70 - Self-Improvement NTS (without Compass labels)

Whenever you use the NTS to view your outer process, you may find a weakness in your approach. The NTS above will help you transform your own weakness into strength. It will also help you extend your attention into your activity, which leads to greater intentionality, insight, and the power to transform.

Wisdom, Knowledge & Understanding

New ideas might appear to belong to the Context Triangle because they come from "outside." It is accurate to say that when we have them, they are part of the material we use to develop our understanding or our creativity. How we "get" new ideas is a different NTS. This next symbol begins when we recognize the need to work with a new idea.

Wisdom develops as we integrate new ideas into our experience. It comes from a transformation of knowledge into understanding. We can increase our knowledge through study, but our understanding comes through experience. And yet, I have met some very experienced people with apparently little wisdom and with far less understanding than was needed for the interactions in which we were involved. Perhaps there was a "disconnect" in their capacity for turning knowledge into understanding. Disconnections can be explained with the NTS just like connections can. Here is a look at how we become wise.

Knowledge into Understanding

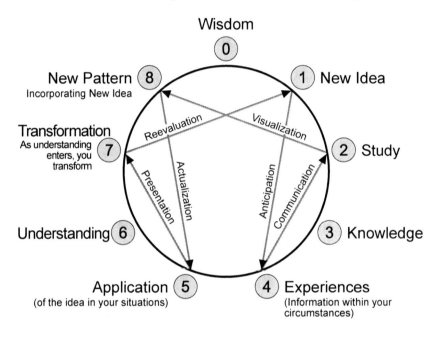

Figure 71 - Wisdom - Transforming Knowledge into Understanding

We can say that we need to <u>look ahead</u> (1-4) into our circumstances to see where a new idea can be used. We look into our information at point 4 to assess where a new idea fits with our existing information. This can't be the end of it—after all, it is a *new* idea, and new ideas require study. Study requires <u>communication</u> during the time the idea is mixing into our experience at point 4. The new idea is now becoming part of our knowledge. Our knowledge affects the way we see our circumstances. It affects the way we see the information we are processing within our experiences (4).

Our study, enhanced by communications coming from observations occurring at point 4, leads us to see a potential—a new pattern that we might be able to use. By <u>visualizing</u> a new pattern, we can <u>actualize</u> a way of applying our new idea at point 5. We will have to repeat this until there are results at point 5. When we actually find that a new pattern is at work in our situations, and it relates to the original new idea—about which we have knowledge—we can move forward.

Once our application works, we <u>present</u> the results of our experiments (5) to our understanding, and if we are aware during this process, our understanding grows, which sends us to point 7. It is here that we can <u>connect back</u> (7-1) with the new idea and see its significance. We see how the idea connects with other ideas. We see how we can continue to put ourselves under the influence of this new idea and how that can provide for our growth. If we have indeed changed, we now see the new idea in a new way—for what it actually does with us rather than what it might do for us. We can call this <u>reevaluation</u> (from our list beginning on page 58 under the title word Restoration).

The new pattern becomes a process we can repeat, which connects us with wisdom. Wisdom is beyond our direct control, but it is reachable through a balance of knowledge and understanding. This balance is an ongoing process and never a fixed bit of information or a gold star on your status report. Within this balance, wisdom can demonstrate the freedom to select from past experience, known patterns or unknown and potential future. The NTS can show us the ingredients that lead to wisdom; we supply the effort. We will look at *how* we can supply the effort in the next chapter.

CHAPTER 13

Use the NTS Like a Magician

In business, as in show business, people play roles. I am in the role of a magician, and you are in the role of CEO: "Chief Extra Officer." All kidding aside, you are in your role. It has a title connected with the form and function you serve. As specialists, we each serve our roles.

Magic is an act. The performer is an actor in the role of "magician." The art of magic, like acting, incorporates body, mind, and emotion. To master the art, one must be able to *direct the intelligences* in one's body, mind, and emotions.

The art of magic demands the use of multiple intelligences on the part of the performer. The *body* conveys subtleties through muscle tension and relaxation. It suggests an empty hand or directs us where to look. The *mind* must have divided attention: aware of both the trick and of how to maintain the appearance of no trick. *Emotions* have a lot to do with acting and presenting. They can convey and elicit sympathetic responses from the audience through the performer's facial expressions, posture, and tone of voice.

The same principles are true for you in your business and personal life. You *must* apply multiple intelligences. How? The NTS shows us what qualities are required of us at each step of a process in which we play a role. It helps us serve our roles. And as we have seen, it can awaken our magical mind to new ideas, encourage us to use our multiple intelligences, and help us bring our attention more fully into our work.

An expert does not become an expert without repetition. In the NTS, the Circle represents the Law of Repetition. By the repeated act of bringing our attention into each step of our expertise, the process of our work evolves. When we bring our attention into the present moment, at each step of our activity, we create the *sensitivity* for new ideas and multiple intelligences.

> As Einstein observed: "It's not that I'm so smart, it's just that I stay with problems longer."

This is an intentional action. We cannot make improvements in our sleep. Although we can dream of potential solutions, we must wake up and get to work to apply them. It is also true that we cannot hold our attention on everything all at once, forever. We need obvious stopping points, rest periods, and points of concentration where we focus our work. With the NTS, we have nine of these points. We use the points around the timeline in order to frame the action of bringing our attention into our process. At point "0/9," the process enters into repetition.

It's not enough to only bring attention into the various points along the way. One has to make new connections between the points of one's process, repeat the connections, and deepen them again and again. This is where the Nine Term Symbol accelerates our development. The inner circulation between the points of an expert's process correlates with the lines of the Compass.

By placing our attention on the Secrets indicated by the inner lines of the Compass rather than only at the stopping points along the Circle Timeline, we establish new connections within the process. What we place our attention on changes in its quality. Remember, the Secrets represent *qualities* that our process must have in order to work efficiently. These qualities come from people, from us playing our roles. We intensify or clarify these qualities by attending to the needs of our expertise. By attending to these needed qualities instead of daydreaming, we establish new connections. **New connections then exist in us as pathways for our creativity**.

It might be useful to picture a business example where new connections were lacking.

Starbucks expanded quickly, and yet "they had us at latte." They were in expansion mode, and they went way past lattes to green tea and panini. Once they offered breakfast sandwiches, they awakened a sleeping giant. As soon as McDonalds offered lattes, Starbucks stock dropped sharply. The founder, Howard Shultz, came back to work at Starbucks to provide something they had lost.

In our language this would be Anticipation, Communication, and Visualization. Starbucks was so busy Actualizing, Presenting, and Restoring—restoring all the way to the bank—that they lost sight of the very trend they had started.

McDonalds poked fun at Starbucks' attitude through their "unsnobby coffee" ad campaign. Starbucks needed to Anticipate the changes that would come when a competitor like McDonalds would serve their primary product: the latte.

A bit of Visualization could have predicted this, and they needed to Communicate about it a year ahead of time. If they had, Starbucks could have been ready for the change with creative new connections emerging from within their business. They could have adapted quickly, if not beat McDonalds to the punch with a less expensive choice.

A whole new invention may be required, but an existing product might do the trick. In fact, I have always enjoyed Starbucks drip coffee. It's less expensive than their lattes, and a simple ad campaign promoting this might stave off McDonalds, and Howard would not be drawn back to work.

The dual action of connecting with the Secrets or qualities circulating through the inner lines of the Compass while bringing attention into the activities at the various points creates an expert—a well connected expert. The inner circulation refers to the repeating pattern of 1-4-2-8-5-7. This is the pattern shown by the Compass. We circulate along these lines when we attend to the Six Secrets while engaging with our activity. We are talking about a way of approaching our expertise (and even learning in general) that creates new neural pathways by intentionally working with our attention.

The best part is that the NTS works without us having to become neural scientists to verify it. Experts love their field, their activities, and their processes, and their love interest naturally draws them into this way of working. It is a natural rhythm visible in symbol through the remarkable patterns of the NTS.

But wait—there's more. The expert also places part of his attention on himself. Why? Because his inner world affects the process too. In our ordinary way of thinking, we do not include ourselves in our equations. Through repetition, the expert finds that his inner states contribute to the process in a variety of ways. His attitude can change the mood of a meeting and affect the productivity of an entire workday. Therefore, he gradually comes to prefer having an awareness of the interconnections, the outer timeline, *and* himself. It is simply more *efficient* this way. Eventually a true expert will choose his inner state in order to effectively function and harmonize with the needs of the process. This is intentionally playing one's role.

I approach my work with an interest in stage presence. To increase stage presence, I practice concentrating my attention within my body while actively engaging in my expertise. Why? Because it is very difficult to simultaneously present a memorized script, emotional moods, and precise physical movements. The script is needed in order to direct people's thoughts; the emotions inspire wonder and enchantment; and the deliberate physical moves accomplish secrets upon which the magic effects rely. It truly requires divided attention and practice, practice, practice. With attention in the body I can experience the dividing of attention that allows me *to intentionally direct all of these at once.*

Imagine you are telling a story to entertain a group of children. Your story is fiction, but you are telling it as though it were true. What if a part of your mind is involved in writing the story at the same time you are speaking it, and every single time you finish a sentence, you automatically shrug your shoulders in punctuation? It would look like you have a nervous twitch. The children might laugh, but it would not be entertaining. When first beginning to perform, magicians unconsciously blink their eyes at the exact moment they "do the secret move." Every magician does this instinctually and must, if he is to progress to the ranks of a pro, find a way to stop the habit. Magic may or may not be done with mirrors, but it certainly is rehearsed in front of one. Magicians blink because it looks more magical when they do not see the move as they watch their effect in the mirror. Of course it looks magical; they weren't watching! If they blink during the move, their magic will look polished during rehearsal but remain flawed in performance. A magician who blinks has not yet learned how to work with his attention—a more closely guarded secret than his secret move.

I found that placing my attention on the inside helped me learn, understand, and repeat complex combinations of body, mind, and feeling. It helped me connect complicated maneuvers with multiple intelligences from the inside out. This same kind of attention exercise is shown to beginning athletes, dancers, and actors. Why not share it with those in business who also seek to accomplish the impossible?

Special attention exercises can be used along with the NTS to greatly increase human effectiveness. That kind of work can culminate in a positive sense of emptiness that allows for creativity, harmony, and freedom. In those moments, it is as if the process unfolds from the center of the NTS rather than its parts. Because these experiences are generally verifiable only with other practitioners in classes or seminars, and they require considerable preparation, I think it's practical to focus here on short-term, noticeable returns like efficiency. Using the NTS, even for gaining an end result, invokes long-term vision that may naturally attract further investigation.

Attention fuels efficiency. The NTS guides our attention within an activity because it shows us where and when to place our attention. During every magic effect I perform, I know when and where to focus. At some points, Restoration is more important than Presentation. At other points, Actualization takes over. The Six Secrets pulsate within every expertise. Success does not happen by magic, but efficiency is magical, and it drives success. It is as impossible to make a process too efficient as it is to stop the success of one that is efficient enough. If you are willing to include the world of attention, I imagine there is no greater tool for connecting all possibilities into the path of efficiency than the Nine Term Symbol.

Roles or Types

We have discussed roles and the qualities that are represented by the Six Secrets. The question arises, what types of roles are needed at each point of the NTS? Can we find a pattern in the type of skills needed at each of the points of the Compass? Of the Context Triangle? My answer to these is yes and no.

As a magician, I aim to inspire people to reach beyond their limits. Even though we want people stationed at each point of our process who can effectively play the roles needed at those points, we do not want to limit a person by defining him or her as a specific "type." People evolve and progress. Some can play multiple roles with unlimited creative skills; others prefer to focus on one expertise.

Different types of people may be more inclined to play certain roles. With this in mind, we can discuss the roles or types that might be useful at or near each point of the NTS. Flexibility is key here, as we are examining "appropriate roles at approximate positions."

Position Roles or Types

Point 1: The Initiator
Point 2: The Planner
Point 4: The Collaborative Worker
Point 5: The Creative Worker
Point 7: The Refiner Finisher
Point 8: The Creator Director

Since what is needed at the Context Triangle is an input coming from outside, the roles at these positions of the Triangle are not definable in the same way. We can say that in every process we have one input that is more *Affirming*, one that is more *Receptive*, and one that is more *Reconciling*. These are qualities with which each participant must interact.

Position Types

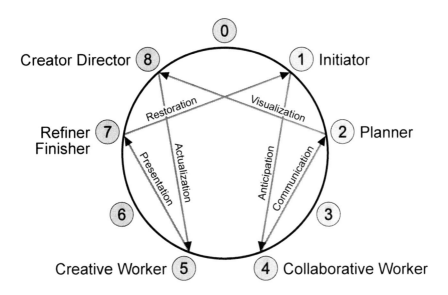

Figure 72 - Types of People - Roles for each Position

Look at your Nine Term Symbol and see if these roles would help your process. In any case, you must keep this question open. What are the most suitable roles for the six positions of your NTS?

Of course, for a group to work together effectively, the Six Secrets must be in fluid circulation, connecting each of these roles at each point or position. This means that the team is applying themselves. Your process cannot have "fluid circulation" without people who are engaged and active. People play the roles at every step of the way. People provide the quality. People make the magic.

To work with roles requires a team that can openly discuss and define their own Position Roles for each NTS they are viewing. The roles above are a starting point for a team to examine. How else could these definitions be used? No one creator/director could possibly assign the perfect person for each role at every position. That would require a psychic. But a group working together can identify useful roles to play at each position.

To appreciate the need for different roles at different positions, to understand another person from within her position, role, or even point of view gives you an immeasurable advantage toward working in synergy with others on a project. The NTS applies to individuals as well as groups. It is a holistic way of thinking about our processes, our roles, how we do things, and how we relate with each other.

Magic Every Day - Aim for the Impossible

When we apply all the lessons of the NTS to our work, it inevitably challenges our limitations. As a magician, this makes me feel right at home. Our idea of what is possible is usually ludicrously limited. We do not know everything about anything. Even a physical object is comprised more of empty space than of solid matter. These ideas are great for magic shows. As my sidekick character in my show *Mysterian* always says, "There is more nothing in something than something in something."

Because we do not know all of the natural, physical, and universal laws that govern our present moment, we can effectively aim beyond what we know to be possible. As the Mysterian says, "We must aim for the impossible in order to find out what is possible." When we picture a future desired result that we do not know to be possible, we are picturing the *potential* future. This might be something we consider impossible by ordinary thinking. But, in fact, the impossible becomes possible. It happens all the time. So we should reach for the stars and be practical at the same time.

Take for example the NTS of a "too busy day." Most people in business do not keep up with every phone call, email, or request for their attention. With the barrage of constant information, it's easy to lose sight of what is important. With our newly developed common language, let's put this into a practical perspective.

The Too Busy Day

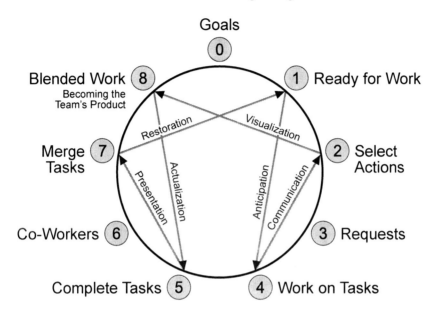

Figure 73 - NTS of the Busy Day

Ready for work, you look ahead or anticipate the tasks already underway. You choose a plan of action based on the pertinent information (communication) about these tasks and their purposes. While you are working on a task, you will refine your selections at point 2 because change is a constant. You are monitoring the requests from others and how the tasks are moving forward. Visualizing the final result (the completed product at point 8) blending into the big picture helps you focus on the important details as you complete a task. It takes a specific kind of concentration (actualization) to bring your tasks to a finished state.

You submit your work (presentation) so it can be used by co-workers. The team now works with your work to steer the outcome, at which point you are free to re-orient and observe (restoration) the results.

Another important aspect of working with the NTS is to have the right qualities operating at the points of the Triangle. For example, what if your Goals are passive when they need to be active? That can cause the system to function slowly. What if the Requests at point 3 are active (first force) when they would best serve as passive (second force)? Then, you might be caught responding to all the requests rather than selecting the ones that need your attention. This is a practical approach to an advanced way of working with the Context Triangle, and it may be useful to review "The Law of Three" section in Chapter 6 to explore this in more depth. It is my experience that the three forces can appear at any one of the points of the Triangle, and that the Context can change with the various configurations of the three forces.

NTS Thinking can be applied in numerous ways to your practical life, your everyday moments, and your business. As we have discussed, it calls us to open our minds and work with our attention. We must bring our attention to the important points of the Circle Timeline and the connections of the Compass to enhance our efficiency and discover the inner qualities we can evoke to play our roles as experts. We also become aware of the role of the Triangle and how the three forces support the whole. Without our attention on specific points, certain connections between the points, and on the whole, the activity returns to evolving by accident rather than through intentionality. Which do you think is more efficient? To aim for the impossible can be as simple as aiming for greater intentionality in our day to day choices.

> In business, problems seem inevitable. I agree with John Lennon when he sings, "I tell them there are no problems, only solutions." But when you know this, the meaning of the word "problem" changes. It is no longer a stopping point, or a place to complain. It becomes a challenge that offers an opportunity. There are plenty of problems in the world. They need our attention; they require our solutions. With the NTS as the mind's tool for looking at problems, solutions appear like magic.

Creativity and Positive Emotions

NTS Thinking is based on a positive psychology that reveals how things are working in a positive light. A failing process does not have a complete NTS. The NTS can show us where to look for the failure, but a complete NTS describes a working scenario. This way of thinking does not try to find out what is wrong—but rather, to find out what is right.

In the magic business, we have a saying: "Pros don't get negative." NTS Thinking leads to a mind that is creative, tolerant, and constructive. It helps you build positive emotions because you know you are moving forward; positive values because you see an overarching purpose; and strength because you can take action at the right time and place in your process.

Positive experiences provide positive emotions and new ways of seeing the world. Wonder is a positive emotion. Experiences that generate positive emotions make negative emotions disappear like magic. This broadens our inner resources. When you become enchanted with your process you create a reservoir of appreciation and understanding that you can draw upon in a crisis or an opportunity. This is a key to reducing stress and building resilience. It is a key to seizing openings for success.

The best systems for understanding processes do not merely fix broken processes, but they help people identify and build their own strengths and virtues within the process. When people exercise personal strengths and virtues within their activities, they generate positive emotions. Lasting happiness, meaning, and purpose result, which in turn leads to solutions and greater efficiency.

Much can be learned from applying the ideas in this book to real situations. Still, there are techniques that cannot be learned only from reading. In this book, I offer some of each. I do not know how to describe what to do to become enchanted with one's process, for instance, but I know it can be an extraordinary experience. It is certainly worth mentioning, as is the need for positive emotion in business. Skilled facilitators, such as the ones listed on the website associated with this book, can use the NTS to lead groups toward these experiences.

Deepening the Secrets

Now that we have developed a common language, and we know how to use the Six Secrets to find solutions within our process-oriented world, it's time to revisit the Six Secrets. Maybe we will become such extraordinary experts at creating solutions that problems can no longer arise in our solution-rich environment.

As promised, we will further elucidate how to use the Six Secrets in NTS Thinking. These descriptions are given without specific processes or examples as **they apply to all completing activities involving change or transformation. Taken together as a whole they reflect a new paradigm for our thinking**.

Secret #1 - Anticipation

You look ahead into the preparation of your work, you scan the details to find needs, gaps, and challenges. The solutions may come into position at any point. The trained eye will see a solution and match it with a need.

The ability to anticipate the needs of a process increases with your understanding. Your understanding grows as you use your attention to follow the new needs of your process while you maintain an awareness of how these needs are being met. Anticipation refers to how you understand the setting up of the conditions that will combine to produce the results of your process. When you look into the conditions that are about to enter into the result, you can ask yourself these questions:

What materials must be present?

What conditions must be present?

What skills do we need?

What training must occur to prepare or compensate?

What details are we leaving unassigned?

What specific conditions are we assuming will be met or are we allowing to be out of our control?

Do we need to make adjustments?

Do we need to make new plans?

What must be communicated to point 2?

Secret #2 - Communication

With attention, you can see the new situation with its new needs, and you can communicate the action of a solution as the process continues.

When you apply solutions, no matter how small they may be, it is communication that moves them toward integration. When a solution must be assigned to a position, communication becomes necessary. Other people or parts of the process must be aware of what is intended.

Communication keeps the attention focused and in line with the intended results and the needs of the present moment.

Secret #3 - Visualization

Imagination is a faculty. It plays a role in making things happen. What people imagine repeatedly will eventually manifest externally in their affairs.

With attention we can train the imaging faculty to find solutions and succeed. People with trained abilities to form images of their aim will more likely actualize that aim.

To train the imagination successfully, you have to observe your thinking. You train your thoughts to picture the end result and to be receptive to new ideas. Picture an infinite intelligence, and this infinite intelligence can send messages, ideas, and images to your mind that help you actualize what you intend.

The word imagination contains the word magician, in the form of "magi." Those who can use the **imag**ing faculty effectively can appear to direct a process from that one "secret" and not need the other five. People who are new to this become astonished when a small wish is fulfilled if it is connected with visualization. They even take this role of Visualization to be the single key to success. It is not. All Six Secrets together are needed.

Secret #4 - Actualization

When you bring your attention to the seeing of new needs—and you stay with those needs until the solution becomes a part of the process—your knowledge becomes complete, and this alone increases your understanding. To actualize a solution is to keep your eye on the ideal solution as you bring the best of what is possible into reality. Actualization is more magical than Visualization. In some ways, it is unexplainable.

The deeper your understanding of the result, of the aim and quality of the experience, the more you can channel the forces and conditions required to actualize the best product.

Secret #5 - Presentation

Each and every detail that goes into preparing a newly actualized result for use by others falls under this heading of Presentation. When you understand how your process becomes more enjoyable, usable, or accessible, you have arrived at the line of Presentation.

Before the product of a process will be used, it is passed to the user through the line of Presentation. The refinements that occur along this line come from direct experience and a concern for ultimate quality. Here, solutions are applied, observed, defined, and refined.

Secret #6 - Restoration

We are constantly bringing chaos into order. Look for ways to prepare to start something or to clean up at the end of something, and you will be looking along this line.

Even the act of summarizing or re-evaluating fits into Restoration. From the most subtle acts of preparation to the obvious movements of restocking, refinancing, and completing, we involve ourselves in Restoration.

Many insights into efficiency come from observing a better way to organize the endings of activities. Through repetition we find deeper and more constructive ways to enhance this part of our process.

Development of Learning

One of the things you can learn from the NTS is a whole new way of approaching the development of learning. Real learning increases your understanding and builds your ability to produce quality, to give, to provide what is needed. A person with these abilities is one with "real being."

Being is difficult to measure, but you can sense it. Some movie stars have it. In fact there are people in all fields with being. It's more than just presence, and one way to get a feel for it in yourself is to look at what and how much you can bear. The more you can accept while remaining in the present moment, the more you can develop or increase your being. People with higher levels of what I am referring to as being can do more than most people imagine. You can even accomplish the impossible if you develop your being.

When something becomes a part of you, you have it forever and you gain from it. It becomes part of your being. We are talking about real experiences that are absorbed into your being through conscious attention. Your attention has to be there in your mind, in your feelings and in your body while you experience new impressions and while you are learning.

This is not an easy skill to attain because our ordinary education is lopsided. Our ordinary education works with information that becomes knowledge. This produces nothing new, but there is another way of working. As new data comes to you, you make a special effort to let it connect with your reasoning. And your reasoning can include all of your parts from your feet to your heart to your head. Through experiencing life with conscious attention in mind, body and heart, you will increase your understanding and develop new whole parts of yourself that remain in your being.

To increase understanding requires you to be there. You can blend with the new data and not simply take it in as information. With this kind of development you become able to bear more, be more, give more and see more. It will be as if you are unstoppable, but not arrogant, because you come from a place of understanding and not merely from your knowledge.

This will assist your groups and teams. Within groups, sharing understanding —concisely and precisely—can lead to greater effectiveness. Groups tend to share only information or knowledge. It is a common notion that knowledge is power. But knowledge is not enough. Knowledge is more effective when it becomes understanding, and even more so when that understanding is shared. There are endless degrees of reason and levels of understanding within a group. The NTS provides a practical way for individuals to share their understanding. When groups deliberately share their understanding, anything is possible, and that is powerful.

When you develop your learning along the lines of the NTS, you develop your understanding and not merely your knowledge. The idea that knowledge is power is an illusion; it is pure fantasy unless it is backed by understanding. Real understanding becomes an inseparable part of you and provides lasting energy for your whole being, whereas increasing your knowledge will only give you more information. Too much information without understanding makes lopsided nerds or off-centered geeks.

Because I learned my art while engaged with the NTS method of learning, the art has become an inseparable part of my being. Due to my specialty of magic, I have developed the instinctive ability, forever a part of my being, to see through deceptive moves—whether physical, psychological, intellectual, or emotional.

I can spot a blackjack dealer dealing seconds. I might not actually see his move, but I will know exactly when he does it. The psychological tricks of advertising and marketing are transparent to my eyes, and I see why people fall prey to the ploys. The ideologies composing political movements do not escape my notice when they suggest promises disguised as a way to get votes.

I wish everyone could be as unaffected by advertising, agendas, angles, and just plain suggestion as a magician. After years of practicing all sides of the art of illusion, I have the beginnings of a unique ability to see through all kinds of deception whether accidental, subtle, or calculated. But I do not think I have become cynical. Most magicians recognize the potential for deception while leaving room for something unknown, unexpected, and unbelievable to enter the scene. I seem to see through deceptions without labeling the situation from a perspective of skepticism, or dismissing it with an attitude of cynicism.

Nothing fools me and yet my life is filled with wonder. I am not overly skeptical because I believe we can accomplish anything our hearts desire. I am not clouded with cynicism because I see all the way through the hints of techniques that cause cynics to have reasonable doubt.

These days, illusionists are in every field. To make money and dominate various markets, people learn tricks to spin webs of false identities. In an age ruled by leaders using deceptive tactics whenever practical, the ability to see—more or less objectively—into the manipulative aspects of all kinds of relationships, while still believing in the wonder of human potential, is a valuable commodity. What does it provide? Besides providing the truth about business choices, contracts, and offers of all kinds, it has led me to see the value in the NTS.

> With the NTS, you can have the same abilities that a magician develops without studying a single trick. You too can see through deceptions like a magician. As a "master of illusion," I recognize the value of the NTS for its ability to cut through all of the incompleteness of a process. And it is in just these points of incompleteness that our illusions lie.

Every magic effect has an incongruity, something that does not follow as it should in reality. The magician must clearly see this and hide it by making it seem irrelevant or appear invisible. There are thousands of techniques for hiding the inconsistency in a magic routine, and a magic routine is nothing other than a process.

With that said, the NTS cuts through lopsided arguments, deceptive business practices, and general misinformation tactics by insisting on clarity and a holistic view. It offers a way to develop real understanding. And as we have just formulated, the increase of understanding leads to higher levels of being, which is exactly what we need if we are going to accomplish anything of lasting quality.

We need more transparency, greater clarity and a true sense of service to the future from all those possessing the power to act effectively in the world today. Serving the future is what is meant by citizenship. Citizenship comes from integrating the third force of the Triangle (the reconciling force) and not permitting the opposing forces to automatically dominate as we saw in Chapter 6. Sure, profits can be made without sustainable evolution, but we aim for more because *we can*. We are capable of efficient relationships that are reciprocal in the way they help maintain one another and sustainable as they guide transformation. The NTS gives a model for all of this. Our role is to be willing to apply it.

The development of learning—the kind of real learning that helps our understanding, and therefore our being, to grow—can be viewed with the Nine Term Symbol. For those skimming the pages of this book looking for information or anecdotal answers to the question of the hour, I imagine this NTS will not be the easiest one to unpack. It pertains to what has been said above about the development of being and connects as well with the NTS of "Transforming Knowledge into Understanding" (page 178).

The phrase NTS Thinking has been used and previously defined. It is through the development of one's learning in this particular way that NTS Thinking becomes more than using information with one's intellect. It becomes conscious thinking with one's whole being. The phrase NTS Thinking is used throughout this book with this specific meaning.

> There is a progression of methods to describe the symbols, aimed at helping the reader develop the ability to use and read an NTS like the one to the right. For example, the methods for referring to the Six Secrets may appear to be inconsistent, and this is because how they are emphasized should change as the material in this book evolves. Sometimes the Six Secrets are underlined and sometimes they are parenthetical, sometimes they begin with a capitalized first letter and sometimes they are all lower case. This is intentional and would ultimately lead to using no emphasis once the parts of the NTS can be recognized within the text of a description without having to point them out. The progression includes being able to read an NTS without an additional description. The "Development of Learning" NTS is a good one for readers to practice relying on the symbol alone for the explanation rather than additional supporting text.

Much can be written about this subject of how we learn. I came to this outline on the next page while studying the "Form and Sequence" chapter in *All & Everything* by G.I. Gurdjieff and by recollecting my own relationship to learning. I have paid close attention to how I learn since I discovered in grade school that learning itself is more fun than what I am learning.

Development of Learning

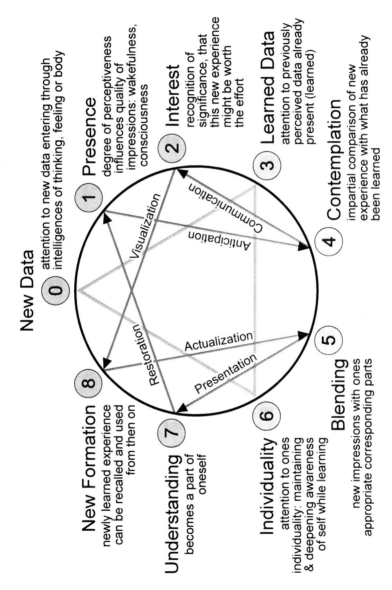

New Data

0 attention to new data entering through intelligences of thinking, feeling or body

1 Presence degree of perceptiveness influences quality of impressions: wakefulness, consciousness

2 Interest recognition of significance, that this new experience might be worth the effort

3 Learned Data attention to previously perceived data already present (learned)

4 Contemplation impartial comparison of new experience with what has already been learned

5 Blending new impressions with ones appropriate corresponding parts

6 Individuality attention to ones individuality: maintaining & deepening awareness of self while learning

7 Understanding becomes a part of oneself

8 New Formation newly learned experience can be recalled and used from then on

Figure 74 - Development of Learning

Realizing Heartfelt Dreams

Attention to the ideas of the NTS and especially the Six Secrets brings a wholeness to our actions that is otherwise lacking. Bringing attention into the present moment is a prerequisite for applying NTS Thinking to our work.

Strength of attention leads to the kind of mental clarity, faith, and determination that can move mountains. Fortunately for me, my predisposition for this way of working was firmly set when an unfortunate accident occurred to my physical body. At the time of a nearly fatal car crash, I had been stagnant in my career, riding on success rather than building my dream show.

A white Camero came out of nowhere, moving sideways at sixty-five miles per hour and taking up both lanes of the country road. Just as suddenly as it appeared, my life was changed. Within a month of learning the true meaning of the word whiplash, and that I would need doctors and a personal injury lawyer, I came to a point of despair. I had lost some of my physical abilities. The right side of my neck, my right arm and hand were in pain with intermittent sensations of numbness. Concurrent with this came the loss of a substantial amount of my financial resources due to a real estate fiasco. My legal fees were growing, and my girlfriend left the country for a job in Europe. I stayed put.

I soon realized that I must work to accomplish my dreams before I used up the time given to me for actualizing my full potential. Although I suffered with severely sprained ligaments, the accident kicked my mind and heart into gear. As a child, I instinctively knew we are capable of more than we could imagine was possible. Years of experimentation brought me to verify that we are not capable of more than we can imagine, but rather of exactly what we can imagine. In other words, we need a strong imagination, the kind artists have, because by actively and repeatedly imagining what we want, we assist the actualization process. We help create what we aim for through visualization. The more vivid, coherent, and constant our imagination becomes, the more likely we are to actualize what we picture in our imagination.

So I put into practice repetition of the visualization of myself reaching my potential and performing specifically intended future manifestations. I had always wanted to build an illusion known as "The Three Minute

Magician." Invented by me and my creative partner, author/illustrator Cooper Edens, this was destined to be the first ever giant hourglass. In the effect, I climb into the top of a 10 foot tall hourglass, close the hatch and ride 180 degrees upside down as the hourglass is turned over by a masked wizard using a giant hand crank. The sand covers me. The hourglass is turned again; the sand runs out; and I am gone, vanished in time. The suspense builds with a series of amazing moments that climax with the masked wizard tearing off his mask to reveal that he is me!

Producing this illusion became my reason for living, and for three years after the accident, I worked intensely toward this aim. I found an Artistic Director at a theatre who liked my material, and with my agreement, they hired a well known playwright to craft the script. With little money of my own, I produced special fundraisers to supply the funds needed to build the expensive effects that no theatre could otherwise afford.

I built the hourglass. It took several years and over $70,000 of R&D, but in the end it became a magical masterpiece. Under my direction, my team of builders and performers combined artistic imagery with sophisticated methods in a new way that had never been done before.

During this process I visualized the end result. My mind's eye could see myself performing this illusion every night in a large theatre. In my mind's ear, I could hear the applause. This is only one of many examples in which I pictured the desired future event and repeated this picturing over and over.

When the Kennedy Center Award winning play that revolved around my original illusions finally opened, I played the role of the magical character appearing in the hourglass at every performance. This was a special version of the effect that was adapted to the story of the play. After the world premiere of this show, my giant hourglass became the centerpiece of *Mysterian*, which played for five years in a theatre built for the show. In this production, I presented an even more amazing version of this spectacular effect in over a thousand performances to dazzled audiences.

It was the combination of the repetition of these visualizations and my application of my understanding of how to effectively work any process that helped me turn my dreams into reality. I worked with all aspects in the world of professional theatre from fundraising to script writing to building effects in the scene shop. I would not have seen how to apply myself effectively to such a wide variety of specialties without NTS Thinking.

With help from many sources, I inspired and created multi-million dollar projects in which my original magic, music, and scripts were centrally featured. I was too busy taking positive steps to be concerned with the fact that only one percent of all the scripts reaching the attention of managing directors in American theatres ever see the light of the stage. I became immersed in outer activities that were required to blend with major organizations, and the Nine Term Symbol helped me prioritize according to principles that benefited each and every process. I was visualizing my desired future results and applying the lessons from the NTS at every important step of the way.

ভ◊ঞ

We lose our connection with wonder too often and too soon. With our connection to wonder goes our belief in ourselves, our potential, and our dreams. When I decided to be a magician, I was too young to understand what a tax form was or why I would need insurance. In other words, I was not filled with doubts. I believed I could succeed, and I headed out to give my magic to the world. It worked. I started a business that eventually took off. I created some spectacular magic and wound up making a living as a performing artist.

It is so unusual that you would think I'd always remember the magic, but as I became successful, I had to reconnect with wonder. I needed the power of creation and transformation in order to actualize my true dreams. The Nine Term Symbol gave me the framework I needed to see the invisible and do what I thought might be impossible. The invisible, of course, is in the qualities of the Six Secrets that I can connect throughout my processes and in the three forces of the Triangle that I must bring together for anything to occur.

My processes were improved due to this. The successes that followed were extraordinary. I produced some of the best magic I could imagine and manifested projects that fulfilled my childhood dreams and artistic visions. I have always felt that as our dreams become reality, this reality helps to keep the world magical.

I am sharing my personal story because it's how I connected with the secrets behind the magic; the depth of real process management—or rather, process miracles. I have tested the NTS and I believe that with NTS Thinking, anyone can connect with the magic of process. Of course accomplishing the impossible doesn't happen without effort. Through efficient, attentive, and intentional repetition, the impossible becomes possible. With the NTS, we have a practical tool, a magical way of thinking, and a guide for working with attention. It is practical in that it gets results, and magical in that intrinsically the NTS preserves a mystery. It shows us how the invisible blends with the visible to actualize everything that evolves, and it puts us right in the midst of it all.

CHAPTER 14

Mastering the NTS in 21 Days

For this chapter, you will need to acquire your own NTS notebook. It should have 100 blank pages. It should be physical, not digital.

In this notebook, for each of the 21 days listed below, you will write detailed notes about your experiences with the suggested activities. By keeping your notes on paper, in one place, you will have a world of connected information by the end of this 21-day period. This will help you verify your insights as your understanding increases and transforms.

After building your NTS on Day 1, you will need to allow for 3-4 pages of notes for each Day. You will probably not use all of that space on any one Day, but you may want to add to that subject at another time, so leave room for future note taking. White space is good. Finding an old note and adding more notes is also good.

Label the top of the page that begins a section with an appropriate heading followed by a brief description of the task, such as: "Day 1—Make My NTS", or "Day 2—Anticipation."

Day 1—Make My NTS

- Pick a process you can work on for the next 21 days.

- Read Chapter 5 again, and produce your own NTS of your selected process. Reviewing Chapter 2 may also be helpful. (Create your NTS on a copy of the blank symbol from page 55, or from one available at accomplishtheimpossible.com.)
- Write today's date on your NTS.
- Place this NTS, with as much detail as you possibly can, at the beginning of your notebook.

Here are some tips to aid you as you work with each of the Six Secrets of your NTS:

You can refer to our ever growing list of "synonyms" on page 58 for help with noting observations about any one of the Six Secrets.

If what you see about a Secret seems trivial, stupid, or ridiculous, write it down anyway. Even if it is only theoretical, write it down.

As for any of these exercises, you can note examples from real experience from any time period. You can even write down what you are imagining, provided it is connected with the line or point you are observing.

Day 2–Anticipation

- Notice times during the day when you are involved in your NTS (in the actual process you have chosen to work with during this period).
- Write down what you see about Anticipation.
- Describe what it means to Anticipate or when you are involved in Anticipation within your NTS.

Day 3–Communication

- Notice, observe, and write down when you are involved with or when your process needs Communication.

Day 4–Visualization

- Focus on Visualization. Make notes.
- No matter how small the detail or how little you see, write it down.

Day 5–Presentation

- Observe Presentation.
- Write your notes. Be specific.

Day 6–Restoration

- Find examples of Restoration. Write these down in detail.

Day 7–Actualization

Time to look at Actualization.
- Write examples of ways you are able to increase your ability to actualize a higher quality within this process.

Day 8–Review and Revise

- Review your NTS.
- Revise it if it has changed.

When revising the NTS, always keep the old one intact and make a second version unless you are only adding to it. Always date any NTS you make, and date your revisions too. It may help to look at a few other processes (on the NTS) from this book or ones you have made up.

Day 9–Weakness

- Pick a weakness or a style of handling your process that comes from you that you want to change, and that you feel could improve the process if it were changed. Be mercilessly honest so you can be sure you have something real.
- Write it down.

Day 10–Examples

- Review the Self-Improvement NTS (see page 175 and page 177).
- Read Chapter 12 again and ask yourself how you can apply the technique to transforming your weakness.
- Write down examples of when your weakness is likely to occur.

Day 11–Bearing

- See if you can bear your weakness and keep looking at it over and over as it occurs in your process.
- Write down the instances when it arises.
- Be specific; resist the urge to adjust. Do not try to change anything.

Day 12–Overlap

This begins a new phase.
- Review your NTS, and ask yourself what other processes connect or overlap with this process.
- Write down any ideas you have about the connections or the manner in which the processes overlap.
- If there is another team that can work with you on this—comprised of folks who already understand this way of working—ask them to join you. They will have to outline their process on the NTS for you

to see by the next day. It is beneficial if their process connects or overlaps with yours, but it does not have to.

The other team can be one individual or a group. If there is no other team, you can play their role in this exercise. If you are playing their role, then you must make up your version of their NTS. Use Chapter 5 as needed to help you make the NTS of their process. Unless you are playing both roles, you do not look at theirs until you are both ready for the next day.

Day 13–Comparing

- Share your NTS with them. Have them share theirs with you.
- Discuss each NTS together, freely, and make notes about what you learn or see.

Day 14–Choosing a Secret

- Pick one of the Six Secrets of your NTS that you wish to strengthen. If what you wish to strengthen contains more than one Secret, that is fine.
- Write this choice down.

Day 15–Strengthening Your Secret

- Work on improving your choice from Day 14.
- Write down each time the improvement comes into focus. This can happen any time there is a moment when this "thing you want to strengthen" shows up as a thought, an observation, a moment of improvement, a moment of weakness, or any other type of manifestation.

Day 16–Repeat

- Repeat the improvement process from Day 15.
- Dig into this as deeply as possible.

Day 17–Sharing Your Secret

- Share the description of your improvement with someone (not your notes from previous days, just the definition of your improvement), and ask them what they think about how you can improve it, or if they see the need for improvement.
- Write down their responses in detail.

Day 18–Review

- Read all of your notes from all of the days above.
- Consider your work, your activity, and your NTS.
- Write down any ideas that come to you about your process.
- Has anything further happened with your work from days 9-11? Review this work, writing down any observations about it.

Day 19–Choosing an Aim

- Ask yourself what is the most important manifestation you wish to achieve over the next year. (The span of time may vary.)
- Write it down.

Day 20–Creating an NTS

- Make an NTS for your choice from Day 19. What will it take for this aim to be realized?

Day 21–Decision

- Ask yourself if you will take on your choice.
- If the answer is "yes," then put the NTS on your wall and consider it every day until you have achieved your aim.
- If your answer is "no," then repeat the activities from Day 19, Day 20 and Day 21 until you have an aim that you really can work on for the next year.

Once you have your aim, use the NTS to make your aim come true. *You* have something special—you know *how*.

Insight & Intrigue

I am enchanted with process and the way the NTS improves business, art, science, and life. I use the NTS to document insights as well as to generate them. I am intrigued with how it functions to help us share ideas, and I remain open to any way of using the symbol that explains anything at all.

Other ways of using this symbol are out there, and some fascinate me. I am especially intrigued by different uses that incorporate the understanding of the math and the laws symbolized in the geometry of the symbol. Much has been written about this symbol, and there is a wealth of information in the complimentary books listed in my recommended reading list at accomplishtheimpossible.com. Within the pages of this book I intentionally remain focused on this particular way of working with the symbol. After all, my research shows that this is the first book to:

- explain the meaning of the lines of the Compass as keys to effectiveness

- show that the connecting lines of the Compass contain aspects of every whole

- reveal how left and right brain thinking unite when you use the symbol

- give a simple method for mapping any process with the NTS

- teach how to make your own symbol for your expertise

- level the playing field by reducing the laws of continuous process improvement to a simple system that anyone can use to transform any process they want

- reveal that the six inner lines depicting the repeating pattern of the Nine Term Symbol are actually the Six Secrets that work in the background of every process and help experts perfect their expertise

In order to integrate the ideas of this system so that they become useful, it is necessary to work with them, and not confuse them with other ways of approaching the symbol. This is why I call the symbol the Nine Term Symbol rather than the enneagram.

G.I. Gurdjieff was the first teacher to use this symbol in modern, verifiable history. His body of work contains writings, dances, music, and methods for working with ideas, multiple intelligences, and attention along with the development of understanding. The way he used the enneagram is astounding. Were it not for his work, the symbol would be unknown. Were it not for his inexplicable way of demonstrating the principles of the symbol through writings, music, and especially in movements, I would not have come to this way of working with process.

Gurdjieff attracted and assisted the development of some very remarkable people who continued to work with his methods throughout their lives and who have influenced me. J.G. Bennett, a student of Gurdjieff's, wrote about using the symbol as a way to deepen our understanding. His insight led to the Six Secrets and to my approach of working with the NTS. I have made efforts to track the first instance of the Six Secrets, but to my knowledge, they were never published, and I have been unable to reach all of my original sources dating back to the early 1980s when I came in contact with Gurdjieff's ideas. I attribute them to J.G. Bennett, but my notes are incomplete, and I am unable to confirm the exact details.

There are many people who have influenced my work, which has led to the existence of this book. It was through personal contact with those who studied with and continued after Gurdjieff that I was aided in my understanding of the ideas in this book. I will not mention all of these helpful people here because, although it is interesting, it does not serve the needs of this material. It is pure magic when people see great ideas—ideas that have the potential to help us in our path of transforming our very essence—and they work to give them to others. I have been a recipient of this action.

Gurdjieff offered the symbol as a tool for people to share specific ideas and develop their understanding. He emphasized just how much can be explained using the symbol when he said, "All knowledge can be included in the enneagram and with the help of the enneagram it can be interpreted. And in this connection only what a man is able to put into the enneagram does he actually know, that is, understand. What he cannot put into the enneagram he does not understand." (*In Search of the Miraculous*, P.D. Ouspensky, page 294.)

Gurdjieff certainly had experience with and understanding of ancient knowledge, and he connected it with his symbol, the enneagram. To the extent each of us connects our understanding, whether ancient or not, with our experience of working with this symbol, we can begin to see how Gurdjieff might have used the enneagram to transmit his experience and understanding. The ideas of three forces (represented by the Context Triangle), the circulation of attention-intention (represented by the Compass), and the transformation of energy (represented by the whole symbol) are unmistakably ancient, and they matter to people in present times. Gurdjieff was able to use the symbol in many different ways to explain these ideas and much more.

It is possible that when we use the NTS, we are getting some benefit from a higher understanding that has been preserved from ancient times. But to imply that this is always true is misleading. Just because the symbol may connect with ancient ideas does not mean that whatever images we can use the symbol to explain are of any ancient significance. We must remember that the present moment is what we can influence. All our work must be connected with the here and now, and although I encourage readers to know there is an ancient and mysterious side to the NTS, I would add that the evidence leads to a study rather than a package of facts.

The historical facts surrounding Gurdjieff and the origination of his symbol do not form a complete picture. Diligent historians have tried to find an instance of this symbol prior to Gurdjieff, but they have not. To dig into this requires a detailed study that is not necessary in order to use the NTS with the Six Secrets. Because working with the NTS as outlined in this book does provide a clear pathway into being able to describe and interpret understanding, I believe this brings us to the here and now.

It should be noted that there are systems displaying the symbol that do not rely on the basic underlying formulations existing within the NTS. I am especially interested in those systems that do use the ideas symbolized by the Context Triangle and the math of the Compass as shown in Chapter 9, "New Way of Thinking." However, my personal interest and focus do not imply rejection of other systems. The fact is that other systems use the same symbol to express intriguing ideas, and it seems logical that they would be compatible. And they may be compatible in some ways even if they do not use the symbol in the same way. This is an important distinction.

For example, the way of working with this symbol that revolves around psychology interests me even though it appears to me that the principles of the symbol are not fully utilized in that system. It reveals a spectrum of personality types and offers insight into personal growth. The very existence of the typology system is an example of how individual experts can use the symbol to express their expertise. Some remarkable ideas have come from this way of working. Although it is unrelated to the system presented here, it is not completely incompatible, as can be seen in the section "Roles or Types" found in this book.

Those interested in this or in the sources of my work can learn more from several books on the aforementioned reading list. For those interested in using the NTS to develop sustainability and transformation within a process, I advise keeping it simple by digging into one's own expertise and deepening one's connection to the methods presented here.

Like most of us, nearly every idea I have seems to come from other people. However, I know of no other simple book like this. I believe a valuable approach to developing one's understanding exists in applying the NTS directly to process work even if it is only for the motive of improvement, and even if it occurs before one studies the enneagram in its original form or its greater complexity. The sources of this work are filled with complex ideas that can distract from one's aim of keeping it simple. I have distilled these ideas to work as a coherent model that maintains the underlying principles of the enneagram. These principles affect us as we work with a form that includes them.

Thanks to many individuals, this book describes a timeless system for process transformation, whole systems development and self-improvement all rolled into one. My wish is that by applying the NTS, readers will acquire a powerful method for increasing efficiency, effectiveness, and creativity derived from an amazing tool. I aim to give NTS users a creativity enhancer, a thinking coach, and an efficiency expert that they can pull out of their hat at will.

If this sounds like magic, it is! As you know, there is a connection to magic throughout this book, but it's illusion-free. Magic is a process-oriented art that depends on simulating and actually mastering material transformations. Magicians aim to amaze people; they never reveal their secrets, and they pay a high price to stay ahead of technology in order to create new effects for modern audiences. Master magicians must, by definition, have a passion for process perfection and be able to see through patterns of deception and suggestion like a psychologist.

This system reveals—without smoke and mirrors—a clear view into the nature of sustainability and transformation. Through the power of the symbol known as the enneagram, we find a new way of thinking that shows how to successfully master every important process.

Finally, the idea that there is a third force that enters into all and everything is challenging for people whether they are in the fields of business, art, science, or life. Working with the NTS and the Six Secrets helps establish patterns that lead to greater understanding of this omnipresent third force. Sustainability and transformation are also complicated subjects to comprehend. The NTS can be approached from a process-action-results-oriented frame of mind and still lead us to a deeper understanding of sustainability and transformation. Even the more invisible ideas contained in the symbol come into focus as we work with what can be seen and what can be done. By doing the small things that we actually can do, we will, eventually, and quite magically, accomplish the impossible.

APPENDIX

Just For Fun: Card Revelations

For the connection to magic to come full circle, I thought I'd leave you with a fun card trick you can use to amaze your friends and create wonder.

Take a deck of cards and choose your favorite card and set it down, face up, in front of you. From the top of the face down deck, deal one card for every letter of your first and last name into a pile. This is called spelling with cards. Now hold this packet of cards in your hands as you picture your magic number. It must be a small number to allow for what is to come, so make sure it is less than half of the number of cards in your hands. You will see why in a moment. Once you have your magic number, deal that number of cards from your packet into a pile. Put this pile of cards that represent your magic number into your pocket.

Now turn your favorite card face down. Count your favorite card as "one," and deal cards from your packet onto your favorite card, one at a time up to your magic number. So, if your magic number is 1, you are done. If it is 2, you deal one more card on top of your favorite card and count "two." Count out loud up to your magic number. Place this packet of cards on top of the remaining cards in your hand and hold them all together.

Spell out your name as you did earlier and transfer one card for every letter of your name from the top of your packet to the bottom. When you have finished, tap the top of the packet and flip over the top card.

You have just used your name and your magic number to find your favorite card. The ritual has been effective, which proves you can do magic.

Due to your smashing success, you are now ready to learn a real card trick. The performance of this next effect can be outlined on the NTS, which makes it super fun.

Your Card and Mine

Take your deck of cards and shuffle it. Cut the deck into two approximately even halves. Place the top half onto a flat surface such as a table, and hold onto the bottom half.

This bottom half is your deck, and the half on the table is the second deck.

Look at the bottom card of your deck and memorize it. Put the deck behind your back and turn it over so that it is face up. Take the top two cards as one, flip them over and place them upside down back onto the top. Bring your deck out from behind your back.

Take the top card from the deck on the table; turn it face up and memorize it. Turn it face down and insert it somewhere near the middle of your deck. You are placing it into your deck in the same direction that the top two cards of your deck are facing.

Take the top card of your deck without looking at its face and insert it into about the middle of the deck on the table. (You might need two hands for this, so you can momentarily place your deck onto the table.)

Hold your deck in one hand and lift off about half of the cards from the deck on the table, flip them over all together, turning them face up (upside down), and place this packet on top of your deck. Flip over the other half of the deck on the table and place this packet under your deck.

All the cards are now back together, but two have been reversed. Tap the deck and spread the cards from hand to hand until you find the two upside down (face down) cards. These are the two cards that you memorized. Was this done by magic? No, but you can make it look like it was.

How quickly you can make this process look like magic will depend a lot on how well you handle cards. While you were following these instructions, if your cards spread all over the place and you could not easily flip over the cards behind your back, or lift one card off the top without exposing the direction of the face up cards underneath, you need some card handling practice.

Imagine being able to flip over the two cards quickly and effortlessly behind your back. Imagine that when you take your top card and place it into the other deck, that none of your cards spread enough to show their direction. These are called "moves."

Let's imagine that you can do those without fumbling the cards. Let's imagine that you have well rehearsed "nice moves." Then you could create a mystery for your friends. Here is how you would present it to make it look and sound like magic:

"Hi, Susan." (Susan is your first victim—I mean, friend—whom you will impress with this effect.) "Would you please shuffle this deck of cards for me? I have something amazing to try with your help."

(She shuffles them.) "Thank you, that is well mixed."

(Lift the deck away from Susan and memorize the bottom card with a quick glance.)

"Take the top half, and do exactly as I do."

(Give her about half of the cards.)

"Cut them a few times or mix them up a little bit behind your back until you have a card on top that you are certain is a random card. Also, this will be a card that you have not yet seen. I will do the same." (Place your deck behind your back and pretend to mix them even more while you reverse the deck and turn the top two cards face down. Square it up and bring it out front.)

"When you are ready, bring your deck out from behind your back. Now take a look at your top card and memorize it. Do not forget this card." (You look at your top card too, but do not memorize it. Instead, recall the bottom card that you already memorized.)

"I will place your card into my deck without looking and you will place my card into your deck."

(Take her top card and insert it into the middle of your deck, being very careful not to expose the direction of your cards. Then, take your top card and place it into her deck near the middle. Once your card is halfway into her deck, you can let her push it in the rest of the way.)

"I will now take about half of your deck and place it on top of my deck, but it will be face up. I will take your other half and place it face up under my deck. So, my deck is the wrong way, sandwiched between the two halves of your deck. The deck is now mixed up with some cards upside down and some cards right side up. With one simple tap, all the cards will align in the same direction. All except two cards: yours and mine. Let's look."

(Spread the deck and show all the cards are face up and two are face down. Your card will be the first one you come to and hers will be the one further down. Make sure to reveal the cards with a sense of drama and mystery. Do not just flip them over. Say yours was the five of hearts, and hers was the six of spades.)

"Here we have one—and look!—here we have another face down card. All the cards are facing the same direction except for these two. And mine is the five of hearts" (flip it face up and act like it is amazing) "and what was yours?" (Make them say it first.) "The six of spades? Wow, look, this one is the six of spades!" (Flip it face up as though it is beyond belief.)

This trick will fool people when it is performed smoothly. What is good about it is that you can do it anywhere with any deck of cards at any time. What is not so good is that you must put the deck behind your back. When I do this for an audience, I do not put the deck behind my back. I flip the bottom card over right in front of them without them seeing it. I also reverse my whole deck without them seeing the move. This makes it more impressive, but being able to do this takes hours of practice.

Now, imagine you are given the task to perform this trick at a cocktail party at which there are 30 people standing in groups of five. You will only do it once, and you would like the whole room to notice that something amazing is happening to the group for which you are performing.

You must anticipate how the deck will come into the scene. Are you supplying it? Is it a borrowed deck? You do not want to offer to perform unless there is a deck of cards easily accessible and unless there is an audience who you feel might listen and follow instructions. You scout the room and anticipate where you can perform so that your back is not in front of a mirror—or, if several groups might turn and watch, you must figure a way to position yourself so you can do your secret moves behind your back without anyone seeing. You cannot adjust later because it would take some of the wonder out of the effect if you were to say, "Please don't watch what I am doing behind my back." You do not even want to say this with body language.

The conditions of the setting and the moods of the different groups will inform you which group to approach. This informing is called communication. You are listening to your audience. Who is in a serious discussion but can be interrupted if it were done tactfully? Who cannot be interrupted at all? Who looks like they would love to see the magic and have a great time?

Once you find your target group, you begin to home in on a possible assistant. If for your helper, you choose the loudest person in the group, you might be in for some surprises. If you pick the quiet, shy person, it will have a different effect. Whom to select as your helper? You have to be sensitive to pick the right group, the right timing, and the best helper. You want a helper who will engage so you can actualize the best reaction. This is the beginning of visualization. If you select the group next to the bar, they may have to move during your performance to let another group get to the bar. If you select the wrong person, the one who does not want to participate, you can end up with their mood negatively affecting the entire experience.

With great concern for the group's final reaction, you begin the procedure. This great concern will help you actualize the best possible results. You present your effect with drama and mystery. You let the group know when the trick is over so that they can go back to their conversation. Going through these steps will involve actualization, presentation, and restoration. If you did not care about the quality of their reaction, you might approach the procedure as just a paint-by-numbers task. But if your livelihood depends on making the group break out into spontaneous applause at the end of your trick, you must ramp up the energy and intensity of your show. This is what is meant by showmanship. You present as best you can, and then you restore the deck to its case (cards cannot get wet or bent or they cannot be used in a trick).

Your Card Trick Performance

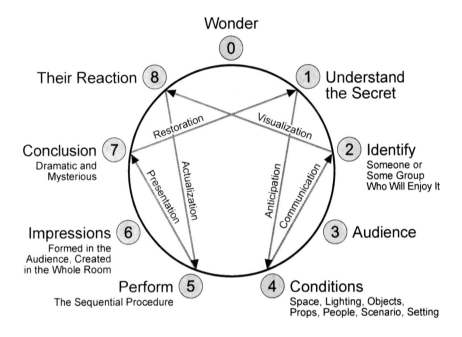

Figure 75 - Your Own Card Trick Performance

Afterwards, then you wonder, was it successful? Was it as complete and awe-inspiring as it could be? What could be improved? All of these answers can be traced on the NTS with its Circle Timeline, Context Triangle and the Compass. The more you repeat both your card trick and your use of the NTS, the better you get at all of these aspects.

It's magic!

Index

Steffan Soule

"Magic does exist. It is created when we
face the unknowable or when we see the
impossible performed right before our eyes."

Steffan Soule is one of the nation's most preeminent magicians and has been recognized with a Kennedy Center Award for the Arts. He has appeared on national television, performed twelve times for Bill Gates, and has put on magic shows for hundreds of corporations nationwide. The Department of Ecology sponsored his show entitled "The Magic of Recycling."

As designer and co-producer of two-million-dollar magic theatres custom built for his shows, Steffan Soule performed the longest running magic show on the West Coast: *Mysterian*. According to magicians, critics, and magic historians, the show's five-year run featured some of the greatest magic in the world.

Steffan and his wife, Barbara, are based in Seattle. He currently performs for theatres, corporate events, and private parties, during which shows an audience member might see his own one hundred-dollar bill vanish from his hand, only to appear embedded in a lemon moments later.

Steffan Soule presents a multimedia experience which gives groups, teams and corporate audiences a practical, stimulating approach to working with the material in this book and to accomplishing the impossible.

Accompanying this Book

AccomplishTheImpossible.com
The Nine Term Symbol (enneagram) is available online at www.accomplishtheimpossible.com. At this site users can create, store, edit and share their own symbols and learn more about using the NTS.

eBook - The Color Version
The eBook of Accomplish the Impossible is available. It is in color with extra features designed to accelerate learning. To purchase the electronic book format, see accomplishtheimpossible.com/ebook

Donations to Sustainability Efforts
A portion of the proceeds from the sale of this book are given to not for profit organizations supporting sustainable business. For more information, see accomplishtheimpossible.com/faq

Online Additions
Visit accomplishtheimpossible.com/firstedition010 to access and print updates and additions to this book as they become available.

CPSIA information can be obtained at www.ICGtesting.com
Printed in the USA
LVOW11s2306060516

486978LV00001B/157/P

9 780984 240517